Daily Lessons from the Saints

DAILY LESSONS FROM THE

SAINTS

52 WEEKS OF INSPIRATION AND ENCOURAGEMENT

FATHER BRICE HIGGINBOTHAM

ROCKRIDGE
PRESS

TRADEMARKS: Rockridge Press and the Rockridge Press logo are trademarks or registered trademarks of Callisto Media Inc. and/or its affiliates, in the United States and other countries, and may not be used without written permission. All other trademarks are the property of their respective owners. Rockridge Press is not associated with any product or vendor mentioned in this book.

Unless otherwise noted, Biblical citations are from the Revised Standard Version—Second Catholic Edition, copyright © 2006 National Council of the Churches of Christ in the United States of America. Used by permission. All rights reserved worldwide. Scripture quotations marked (NABRE) are taken from the New American Bible, revised edition © 2010, 1991, 1986, 1970 Confraternity of Christian Doctrine, Washington, D.C. and are used by permission of the copyright owner. All Rights Reserved. No part of the New American Bible may be reproduced in any form without permission in writing from the copyright owner.

"Litany of Trust" by Sr. Faustina Maria Pia, SV. Used by permission of the Sisters of Life. www.sistersoflife.org.

Nihil Obstat: Reverend Joshua J. Rodrigue, STL, Censor Librorum
August 11, 2020

Imprimatur: † Most Reverend Shelton J. Fabre, Bishop of Houma-Thibodaux
August 11, 2020

The *Nihil Obstat* and *Imprimatur* are official declarations that a book or pamphlet is free of doctrinal or moral error. No implication is contained therein that those who have granted the *Nihil Obstat* or *Imprimatur* agree with the content, opinions, or statements expressed.

Interior and Cover Designer: Antonio Valverde and Erik Jacobsen
Art Producer: Tom Hood
Editor: Lauren O'Neal and Carolyn Abate
Production Manager: Jose Olivera
Production Editor: Ashley Polikoff
Illustration © Clairice Gifford, 2020
Author photo courtesy Tyler Neil and the Diocese of Houma-Thibodaux

ISBN: Print 978-1-64739-747-0
eBook 978-1-64739-449-3
R1

To my friends who have walked with me
on the path of sainthood, especially
Jen, John David, Kent, Addy, Mary,
Josh, Hayden, Chase, Natalie, and Parker.

Contents

INTRODUCTION

Welcome to our journey to Jesus with the saints!

As a Christian since receiving the gift of baptism at 10 days old, I have been abundantly blessed by the intercession and example of the "great cloud of witnesses" to "run with perseverance the race that is set before us" (Hebrews 12:1). As a Catholic priest, I have seen over and over again how necessary it is for disciples of Jesus to travel with other disciples if we're going to persevere in "looking to Jesus the pioneer and perfecter of our faith" (Hebrews 12:2).

So what is a saint? Derived from the Latin word *sanctus*, its most basic definition is simply someone who is holy. The Bible actually most often uses it to refer to people like you and me—baptized Christians who are living in God's grace and thereby traveling toward heaven—as well as those who have actually made it to heaven (the most common use of the term today).

In addition, there are the canonized saints we'll walk with in this book. Canonization happens when the pope declares, as the glossary of the *Catechism of the Catholic Church* states, that "a deceased [Christian] may be proposed as a model and intercessor to the Christian faithful and venerated as a saint" if "the person lived a life of heroic virtue or remained faithful to God through martyrdom." When a saint is canonized, our mother the Church assures us that this person is both in heaven and a good example for us to imitate. This means that, in the liturgy, we can both honor the saint and ask for his or her intercession.

In our personal prayer, we can also ask those who have died but are *not* canonized to pray for us. But we want to pray for them, too, in case they're being prepared for heaven in purgatory. I love stopping by the local graveyard during the day to pray. When I do, I ask all of those whose bodies are buried there who have made it to heaven to pray for me, and I pray for those whose bodies are buried there who are being prepared for heaven by the purification of purgatory.

We need Christian friends on earth, and we need Christian friends in heaven. "The prayer of a righteous man has great power in its effects" (James 5:16), and those friends of ours who have already made it to heaven are certainly the most righteous. The purpose of this book is to help each of us walk with the canonized saints so that we can better imitate their virtues and ask for their help in living as saints ourselves today on earth. Together, let's get to know these friends in heaven. May we take inspiration from their example, learn from their practices, and depend on their intercession as we strive to enter through the narrow gate of heaven by the grace of God (Matthew 7:13–14) and thereby become saints ourselves.

How to Use This Book

This book is designed to be first of all *practical*—to actually help you in your daily life. Each week is focused on one saint—one member of the "cloud of witnesses" (Hebrews 12:1) that instructs, inspires, and intercedes for us. Each day contains a lesson or practice inspired by that week's saint, which will help you live more like a saint yourself. Each day's reading takes less than five minutes, but if you apply the lessons you learn, you'll reap the benefits throughout your entire day.

We'll roughly follow the liturgical calendar, so if you begin with week 1 on the Sunday before January 1, you'll be learning about each saint at more or less the same time we remember him or her together as the Church—sometimes a little before or after. However, it ultimately doesn't matter when you start reading or whether you're reading about a given saint on his or her feast day; you can learn valuable lessons from any saint on any day of the year. If you miss a day or a week, don't worry. Just catch up when you can. The most important thing isn't to finish the book "perfectly." The most important thing is to live what you learn. Five minutes a day can change your life! So let's get started.

Mary, Queen of All Saints

Mother of God, Queen of All Saints

Mother of All Peoples

FEAST DAY: Multiple, but January 1 is the Feast (Solemnity) of Mary, Mother of God, her most fundamental title.

DAY 1

On the heels of Christmas, we continue to reflect on the manger scene, in which we encounter not just the child Jesus but also Mary, Joseph, the animals, the shepherds, and, after a while, even the wise men. Jesus is obviously the most important person in the manger scene, but who is the *second* most important person there? Mary, His mother!

✝ We all have many memories of Christmas—memories of family, food, presents, and the rest. When you think of Christmas, what makes you think of Jesus? Spend a few moments today thanking God for that memory.

DAY 2

Why do we love Mary so much? Why do we Catholics give her so much honor? The answer is this: Imagine you had the opportunity to create your own mother. Imagine how you would make her. Imagine how much you would want to preserve her from anything bad, from anything evil, from anything wicked. That is Mary.

† Think about your mother today. How has her life blessed you? Where does she need your prayers? Offer a prayer to God today for your mother.

DAY 3

We honor Mary because she is the Mother of God. We honor Mary because Jesus honors Mary in creating her. Everything we believe about Mary comes from the fundamental truth that she is the Mother of God the Son and that she is therefore the mother of us—everything we believe about Mary is based on or protects that which we believe about Jesus.

† Open your Bible to Matthew 1:18–2:23. What do you think it was like for Mary and Joseph to talk about this baby having been conceived miraculously? To receive the visit of the wise men, to fly by night into Egypt, to return to Nazareth? Imagine yourself in one of these scenes. What might God be teaching you through this scene?

DAY 4

In the Bible, St. Paul remembers St. Timothy's sincere faith, "a faith that dwelt first in your grandmother Lois and your mother Eunice and now, I am sure, dwells in you" (2 Timothy 1:5). Like Lois and Eunice mothered Timothy, Mary must surely have prayed with Jesus and remembered the Scriptures with Him.

† Who do you consider a spiritual parent? Who in the Church has handed on the faith to you? Who in the Church has taught you about the Bible? Which family members? Which priests or deacons or bishops? Remember their teaching and thank God for them today.

DAY 5

Remember the wedding at Cana in John 2? Mary says to the servants the same thing she says to you and to me today: "Do whatever He tells you" (John 2:5). She will help us always look to Him. By being who she is, she teaches us about Jesus. And that's why we say, echoing the words of Gabriel in the Gospel of Luke, "Hail [Mary], full of grace, the Lord is with you!" (Luke 1:28). And that's why we ask her, with all of our hearts, "Please pray for us—we who are sinners—now and at the hour of our death. Amen."

† Open your Bible today. Read Luke 1:28, 42. This is the first half of the Hail Mary prayer. Ask Jesus to teach you the right way to see Mary today. Ask Him to teach you how to see her through Gabriel's eyes, Elizabeth's eyes, and His own eyes.

DAY 6

After Jesus was crucified, Mary lived in a city called Ephesus in what is now Turkey, alongside St. John the Apostle and Evangelist, who was bishop there, until the end of her days. In AD 431, all the bishops of the world—or most of them—gathered in Ephesus to talk about Jesus and the nature of His humanity and divinity. Places are important. It was fitting that debates about Jesus's nature would be held in the place where Mary and St. John had lived.

† Which places are important to your walk with Jesus? Maybe there's a place at your house or in your town where you've had profound encounters with God. Go back there soon, physically or in your imagination. Thank God for that experience. Rest in the grace of the past. Then ask Jesus if He has any deeper graces for you in the present.

DAY 7

At the Council of Ephesus, someone said that Jesus was really two persons—not one person with a human nature and a divine nature, but two persons in one body. The bishops, led by St. Cyril of Alexandria, said no. The Bible and the tradition of the Church teach us that Jesus is one person—fully God and fully man. And that means the mother whom He created for Himself can truly be called Mother of God. And that's why we honor Mary so deeply—because she bears God to us, because she brings God to us, because she points always to Jesus.

† The truth that Jesus is one divine person who has both a human and a divine nature is fundamental to our lives as Christians. And Mary, the Mother of God, surrounds, protects, and elucidates that truth. This is Mary's vocation: to mother, to protect, and to bear forth Jesus. Having been given as mother to all of Jesus's disciples at the foot of the cross (John 19:25–27), she also mothers us. Remembering that Jesus has given her to us as our mother, too, ask Mary for help in those places where you need help today.

WEEK 2

St. Basil & St. Gregory

Bishops and Doctors of the Church

Patron saints of education, exorcisms, liturgists, and monks, among others

FEAST DAY: January 2

DAY 1

We take our next step on our journey with our friends in heaven by turning toward two great saints who were friends on earth: St. Basil the Great and St. Gregory of Nazianzus. There's a saying that "saints come in pairs." When Jesus sent forth His disciples to prepare the way for His coming, He sent them "two by two" (Luke 10:1, Mark 6:7). They were able to lean on and support one another.

† Who is in your support network? Who can you lean on when things get tough and rejoice with when things are good? Who knows your struggles well enough to support you when you're down and to call you higher when you sin? If you don't have someone like this in your life, ask Jesus to bring a best friend into your life, and ask Basil and Gregory to pray for you.

DAY 2

Both Basil and Gregory were blessed with families devoted to goodness and holiness. Basil came from a family of saints, including his parents, Basil the Elder and Emmelia of Caesarea. His brothers and sisters—both those who were married and those who were consecrated to God—were all renowned for their piety. Basil's eldest sister, Macrina, and two of his brothers, Gregory of Nyssa and Peter of Sebaste, are also officially numbered among the saints. Gregory's parents are, too—his father, also named Gregory, and his mother, Nonna.

† Most of our families are not as saint-filled as these families, but most of our families do contain saintly examples. Who in your family is a holy example for you? Think of one of his or her virtues and put it into practice this week.

DAY 3

Both born and raised in the region of Cappadocia (in what is now Turkey), Basil and Gregory both found themselves in Athens for studies, where the spark of the acquaintance they'd made in Basil's hometown of Caesarea was fanned into a flame of deep friendship. Gregory himself said, "We had come, like streams of a river, from the same source in our native land, had separated from each other in pursuit of learning, and were now united again as if by plan, for God so arranged it."

† Who among your acquaintances might be able to become this kind of friend? Someone at church? At work? Talk to that person. Grab coffee together. See if there's potential for a deeper friendship.

DAY 4

The ancient philosopher Aristotle said that friendship can be based on utility, enjoyment, or virtue. Friendships based on utility are like business arrangements, while those based on enjoyment might include either wholesome diversions or sinful ones. Both are self-focused, depending on people's usefulness to each other or their enjoyment of their time together. Friendships based on virtue, on the other hand, are complete or perfect friendships, wherein two people focus on each other's good. Gregory wrote, "The same hope inspired us: the pursuit of learning. This is an ambition especially subject to envy. Yet between us there was no envy. On the contrary, we made capital out of our rivalry. Our rivalry consisted, not in seeking the first place for oneself but in yielding it to the other, for we each looked on the other's success as his own."

† Thank God today for the friends with whom you have virtuous friendships.

DAY 5

These days, the concept of intimacy between friends is nearly lost. But to Gregory and Basil, such pure and holy friendship was "that flame that was to bind us together . . . When, in the course of time, we acknowledged our friendship and recognized that our ambition was a life of true wisdom, we became everything to each other." Basil and Gregory were together in pursuit of learning, God, and virtue. Their brotherly love spurred each on to sainthood, a sanctity that often "comes in pairs."

† How do you normally respond to invitations into the intimacy of friendship? Can you talk to your friends (or at least a few of them) about the deep things of life? Your aspirations? Your goals? Your relationship with God?

DAY 6

Basil is sometimes called the "Father of Eastern Monasticism." Having spent time as a monk himself, he supervised monasteries of both men and women, even after becoming a bishop. His guidance for monks and nuns is still followed in many parts of the world today. For Gregory's part, he taught St. Jerome, the great Bible scholar, and presided over the Council of Constantinople, which finalized the Nicene Creed we proclaim each Sunday at Mass. Their lives continue to influence the daily lives of all Christians today.

✝ How can you influence the lives of others? Can you give a bit of time to mentor someone personally?

DAY 7

On this final day of our reflections on the dear friends Basil and Gregory, let us allow ourselves to be mentored by the writings of Basil regarding something most of us struggle with: anger and unforgiveness. "Do not overturn your own purpose, and do not appear to be easily accessible to those who insult you," he wrote. "Let him bark at you ineffectually; let it burst upon himself. For the one who strikes one who feels no pain takes vengeance on himself, for neither is his enemy repaid, nor is his temper assuaged. Likewise, the person reproaching one unaffected by abuse is unable to find relief for his passion. On the contrary, as I have said, he is indeed cut to the heart."

✝ Basil puts our temptations to anger and unforgiveness into perspective. How can thinking with a different perspective change our day-to-day actions?

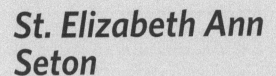

WEEK 3

St. Elizabeth Ann Seton

Religious sister and founder of the Sisters of Charity

Patron saint of Catholic schools, seafarers, widows, and the state of Maryland

FEAST DAY: January 4

DAY 1

On September 14, 1975, Pope St. Paul VI canonized Elizabeth Ann Seton, officially declaring her a saint. "Canonize" is the verb we use to say that someone has been officially declared to be a saint and added to the "canon," or official listing of recognized saints of the Church. A saint is any person in heaven or, even more broadly, anyone who has received the gift of baptism (1 Corinthians 1:2). But what does it take to be officially declared a saint? Two things: heroic virtue and evidence of effective prayers after death. Every officially declared saint has shown in his or her life some great virtue.

† Though you may not be called to canonization, you are called to be a saint. That means that God has both destined and empowered you and me, by the gift of baptism, to live with heroic virtue. What is one virtue in which God might be calling you to grow right now?

DAY 2

As James 5:16 says, "the prayer of a righteous person has great power in its effects." After a person who has shown heroic virtue dies, people who knew the person will often begin to ask for prayers. The idea is: *If she was really close to God on earth, then she must be in heaven. If she's in heaven, then she's even closer to God. So I'll keep asking her to pray for me.* By the time Elizabeth died, her life spoke clearly of her heroic virtue, and those who knew her began to ask her to pray for them from heaven. If this person's intercession is proven through two scientifically verified miracles, the saint is canonized, and his or her name is allowed to be used in liturgy—in public worship—as an intercessor before the throne of God.

† Do you know someone in your life, now passed away, who lived with heroic virtue? Say a prayer for that person, asking God in His mercy to bring him or her into heaven. Then ask him or her to pray for you: "_____, if you are in heaven with Jesus right now, please pray for me. Please ask Jesus our Lord to help me with _____."

DAY 3

Born in New York in 1774, Elizabeth was the first person from what is now the United States to be canonized. In his homily at her canonization, Pope St. Paul VI proclaimed, "St. Elizabeth Ann Seton is an American. All of us say this with spiritual joy, and with the intention of honoring the land and the nation from which she marvelously sprang forth as the first flower in the calendar of the saints . . . Rejoice, we say to the great nation of the United States of America. Rejoice for your glorious daughter."

† Every culture that has ever arisen has both great virtues and terrible vices. What is one virtue present in your culture that you'd like to cultivate in yourself? Perhaps it's one present in American ideals, such as hard work, freedom, or patriotism. How can you cultivate this virtue in your own life?

DAY 4

As a religious sister, Elizabeth served the poor of the United States. In such a prosperous land, she encountered the opposite of prosperity, and her heart was moved with the love of Jesus, who invited her to care for the "least of these" (Matthew 25:40). From this desire in her own heart—having been both rich and poor in her lifetime—Elizabeth began the Catholic school movement in America by offering the country's first free Catholic school, in Emmitsburg, Maryland.

† In a society marked by individualism, Elizabeth chose to practice the virtue of interdependent solidarity—what Pope St. John Paul II called "a firm and persevering determination to commit oneself to the common good. That is to say to the good of all and of each individual, because we are all really responsible for all." Let us imitate Elizabeth in the practice of this important virtue of solidarity. We could do so by spending time with those who are lonely, providing for the needs of the poor, or using our knowledge to help those who struggle in school.

DAY 5

In a saint's life, we're sure to find suffering. If, as Mother Teresa said, "suffering[s] are but the kiss of Jesus," then we shouldn't be surprised when the saints receive many such kisses. Jesus suffered much, and He gives us the gift of being like Him in our sufferings. One such suffering in the life of Elizabeth was her husband William's tuberculosis. During perilous economic times, the stress on William worsened this disease, so he, Elizabeth, and their eldest daughter traveled to Italy in hopes that the Italian climate would bolster his health. However, William died in Italy shortly after their arrival.

† Thank Jesus for one kiss you have received from Him recently in the form of suffering. Ask Him to use this to help you become a saint (whether you're ever canonized or not).

DAY 6

Stranded in Italy after her husband's death, Elizabeth and her daughter Anna Maria were taken in by her late husband's Italian business partners. The great charity of the devout Filicchi family provided a vibrant example of Catholic life that greatly attracted Elizabeth, who had been raised Anglican. Struggling with the movements in her heart and mind to convert to Catholicism, she prayed a portion of "The Universal Prayer" by Alexander Pope: "If I am right, Thy grace impart, still in the right to stay; If I am wrong, O, teach my heart to find that better way." With sincere prayer as well as fasting, Elizabeth became Catholic on Ash Wednesday, 1805, and received her first Communion on March 25.

† Thank God today for someone who has shown you the love of Jesus, especially when you were down and out, as the Filicchi family did for Elizabeth.

DAY 7

Converting to Catholicism in the early 1800s in New York was a socially momentous move. Elizabeth knew that, with this decision, she would lose much support and economic opportunity. Yet she made the courageous decision to follow her conscience, which had been convicted of the truth that the Church Jesus founded (Matthew 16:18–20) truly subsists in the Catholic Church and nowhere else.

† Convert or not—Catholic or not—we will each face persecution if we are serious about living the gospel (Matthew 10:24-25). Where can you follow Elizabeth's example of courage? Do you need to stand up more for those who are being gossiped about? Do you need to study more about your faith to respond to challenges from others? How can you be courageous in living and spreading the faith that has been gifted to you?

St. Anthony of the Desert

Abbot

Patron saint of monks, butchers, those with skin conditions, and basket weavers

FEAST DAY: January 17

DAY 1

Anthony was born to wealthy parents in Egypt during the middle of the third century. They died when Anthony was about 20 years old, leaving him with significant wealth—and a responsibility to take care of his younger sister. When he became a monk, Anthony disposed of the bulk of his riches, keeping only enough to care for his sister, and devoted himself to prayer and fasting. The virtue of prudence, also called "practical wisdom," is knowing the particular good for particular circumstances. Although Anthony knew that God was calling him to total devotion, he knew he had a duty to care for his sister, too.

† The Old Testament books of Proverbs, Wisdom, and Sirach are treasuries of practical wisdom. Consider reading a page or two of one of these books. Chapters 7 and 8 of the Book of Wisdom teach what wisdom is and how to get it. Proverbs 31 beautifully extols the virtuous woman. And Sirach 2—one of my favorite chapters in the whole Bible—teaches a disciple how to follow the Lord, especially when trials and tribulations come up.

DAY 2

It was during a visit to his local church that Anthony received his call. Coming to pray in the local church one day, he heard the words of Jesus to the rich young man: "If you would be perfect, go, sell what you possess and give to the poor, and you will have treasure in heaven; and come, follow me" (Matthew 19:21). Anthony took these words to heart as being spoken directly by God to himself.

† The *Catechism of the Catholic Church* quotes the Second Vatican Council: "In the sacred books, the Father who is in heaven comes lovingly to meet his children, and talks with them." Through the Bible, God wants to talk *to you* like He did to Anthony. Read the Bible for five minutes today. Maybe begin with the book of Psalms or Proverbs. Ask, "Father, what are You saying *to me* through the Scriptures today?"

DAY 3

At this time, the life of monks consisted, like it does today, of celibacy, prayer, sacrifice, and good works. But these monks of old most often continued living in their homes with their families. Around the time Anthony was alive, some monks began to move away from their homes, instead living in huts or caves. After visiting these monks, studying their lives, and learning all that he could from them, Anthony himself took up residence in a cave on the outskirts of the city.

† We are not all called to be monks. However, all Christians are called to a different kind of life than those who are of the world (see John 17:16). How should your life as a Christian look different from the life of someone who does not believe in Christ?

DAY 4

After 15 years, Anthony, now 35 years old, had a great desire for communion with Jesus that led him to the total isolation of the desert. For 20 years, he remained alone there, deepening his relationship with God. Human beings are never satisfied. We always want bigger or better or more. Why? We are never satisfied because we were made with an infinite desire, a longing that only infinity can satisfy. Even though Anthony was a monk, he wanted more. He desired to drink more deeply of the infinite.

† Where can you make more room in your life for the infinite? Maybe it's just five more minutes of prayer a day. Maybe it's one less snack, taking your mind away from the things of the world, like food, and directing it to the supernatural.

DAY 5

Over the course of his life, Anthony was afflicted by the devil with many temptations—laziness, lust, pride, and even physical demonic attacks meant to discourage him. Anthony, however, refused to give up. Instead, he said to the multiple demons who tormented him, "If any of you have any authority over me, only one would have been enough to fight me." At that, they disappeared like smoke. Anthony knew that, having become a Christian through the grace of baptism, the only way that the devil could hurt him was if he chose to sin.

† Where does the devil tempt you? Have you chosen to sin? To commit even a mortal sin (1 John 5:16)? Beg God for forgiveness. Go to confession at your local parish. Then, living in the grace of your Christian life, contend like Anthony with the tempting demons: "I am a Christian. You have no authority over me."

DAY 6

As time passed, Anthony's holiness became so renowned that other monks began living in nearby caves, begging him to come forth from his seclusion and guide them in their own walks with God. Eventually, Anthony acquiesced. Emerging from his retreat, he spent five or six years teaching and organizing this community of monks. Then he went back to being a hermit for the last 45 years of his life, but he freely received visitors who approached him for guidance, and he sometimes traveled to the city to provide wisdom to the people there. He embraced mentoring others.

† Who has been a mentor in your life, teaching you the ways of holiness? Thank God for that person today. If you can, drop a note to your mentor thanking him or her personally.

DAY 7

The wisdom of these ancient monks of the desert (often called the Desert Fathers) is preserved mostly in short stories or sayings. One such story tells that someone once asked Anthony, "What ought I to do?" The saint replied, "Do not trust in your own righteousness and do not worry about the past, but control your tongue and your stomach."

† Often we make things too complicated. If we could heed the simple wisdom of wise men and women who came before us, we would find that the path to happiness is simpler than we often think. Following the advice of Anthony, substitute good words for gossip and fasting for feasting. You will surely find greater happiness.

St. Francis de Sales

Bishop and Doctor of the Church

Patron saint of writers, journalists, educators, deaf people, and the Diocese of Houma-Thibodaux in Louisiana, among others

FEAST DAY: January 24

DAY 1

Young Francis de Sales was sent by his father, who wanted him to go into politics, to receive an excellent education in the city of Paris. While there, Francis began to study theology. He also fell into deep despair. Would he be saved? Could he ever manage to go to heaven? Plagued by fear of hell, he turned to the intercession of the Blessed Virgin Mary. After asking for her help, he found his despair had disappeared. He dedicated himself to Jesus through Mary, making a vow of chastity out of deep and exclusive love for God, who is love itself (1 John 4:16).

† Open up your Bible today. Read 1 John 4:7–21. Read it slowly. Read it twice. Read it aloud. What word or phrase strikes you? Spend some time thinking about whatever stands out to you. Then tell God what you're thinking or feeling.

DAY 2

Having completed doctoral studies in both law and theology, Francis was determined to become a priest. His father, however, had different plans; he had arranged for Francis to take various prestigious positions and marry a noblewoman. The bishop, however, interceded with Francis's father on his behalf, and Francis was ordained to the priesthood in 1593.

† Francis chose to follow the path on which he clearly discerned that God was inviting him. He refused to let anything get in his way, even the intense external pressure from his father. What is the biggest obstacle to your fulfillment in your life right now? What realistic step could you take to move toward that joy of fulfillment? Take one small step toward joy this week.

DAY 3

As a priest, Francis was immediately given the job of provost, the highest position in the diocese after that of bishop. As provost, Francis supervised other priests and engaged in zealous evangelical work—preaching, hearing confessions, and distributing pamphlets explaining the teachings of the Catholic Church. Francis had a great circle of influence, and he faithfully used his influence to give of himself and to preach the gospel. This fidelity led him to receiving even greater influence; after nine years as priest and provost, Francis became bishop of Geneva in Switzerland in 1602.

† What is your circle of influence? What is one way in which you can be faithful with that which has been entrusted to you?

DAY 4

Although he was its bishop, Francis couldn't reside in Geneva because it remained controlled by Calvinists. Nonetheless, Francis worked tirelessly for their conversion and formed relationships with a significant number of Calvinists. He also fostered collaboration within the Church to lead a diocese filled with dedicated clergy and well-educated laypeople. He was a successful relationship builder. The phrase "A spoonful of honey attracts more flies than a barrelful of vinegar," often attributed to Francis, remains in use in various forms to this day.

† Francis's position as provost, then as bishop, certainly gave him some influence. But most of his influence came from his *character*, not from his position. He chose to exhibit kindness and love to all people, even those he disagreed with. Who is someone in your life you disagree with? First, pray for them. Second, fast for them. And third, think of some external act of kindness you can do for them—a kind word, a little note, or an act of service.

DAY 5

Although Francis was naturally quick-tempered, he worked for 20 years to conquer this vice and is today so known for his meekness that he is called the "gentleman saint."

† What is your greatest vice or flaw? This is commonly called a "predominant fault," and everyone has one. Make a plan to conquer this flaw. Ask a wise spiritual person in your life to help you and a good friend to keep you accountable.

DAY 6

Francis worked closely with a branch of the religious order founded by another Francis: St. Francis of Assisi's Order of Friars Minor Capuchin. He also collaborated with his dear friend, Jane Frances de Chantal, to found the Sisters of the Visitation of Holy Mary. Today, their relics can be found together in the Basilica of the Visitation in Annecy, France.

✝ Two days ago, we thought of those with whom we disagree. But what about those who are very close to you? Sometimes it's easy to ignore those closest to us because "they'll always be there." What is one way that you can show love and kindness today to at least one person whom you dearly love?

DAY 7

Francis is patron saint of writers and journalists because he made extensive use of pamphlets and books—the dominant communications technologies at that time—to spread the faith. He is patron saint of the deaf because he once developed a sign language to teach a deaf man about God.

✝ Francis used everything at his disposal to preach the gospel. What tools and skills do you have at your disposal? (For example, do you use social media to glorify God and build up others, or do you use it for detraction and gossip?)

St. Simeon & St. Anna

Prophets

Patron saints of the elderly; Anna is a patron saint of consecrated widows

FEAST DAY: February 3 (on some calendars)

DAY 1

February 3 honors two biblical saints: Simeon and Anna. Forty days after the birth of Jesus, he was taken to the temple by Mary and Joseph to be presented to the Father (Luke 2:22–24). There at the temple, they met Simeon, a "righteous and devout" man (2:25), and Anna, an 84-year-old prophet and widow. As we celebrate December 25 as the date of Jesus's birth, 40 days after that is February 2, the Feast of the Presentation of the Lord. Simeon and Anna, who figure prominently in this historical event, are therefore celebrated together on the very next day.

† We celebrate anniversaries, birthdays, and the like with fond memories and great joy. So, too, the whole Church celebrates together these important days in the life of our Savior!

DAY 2

As with Mary, whose feast days highlight the mysteries of Christ's life, so too with all the saints. The life of each saint is an expression of the "many-sided wisdom of God" (Ephesians 3:10, author's translation) by which His glory is magnified on earth. Each Christian is called to become a saint—called to live the kind of life that shows others the deep and abiding love of Christ. We are each called to be able to say with St. Paul, "Be imitators of me, as I am of Christ" (1 Corinthians 11:1)!

† The memory of Simeon and Anna is defined by their encounter with Jesus Christ. How is your life defined by your encounters with Jesus?

DAY 3

Simeon was in touch with the Holy Spirit. The Bible says that he was "looking for the consolation of Israel, and the Holy Spirit was upon him" (Luke 2:25). The Greek word for "consolation" here is *paraklēsis*, a word that might be familiar to you if you've ever heard the Holy Spirit called the "Paraclete." By noting Simeon's focus on the consolation (*paraklēsis*) of Israel and then immediately mentioning the Holy Spirit, the Scriptures indicate to us that Simeon was focused on the Holy Spirit.

† Ask for the Holy Spirit to guide you this day. Feel free to use your own words, or try these: "Come, Holy Spirit, fill the hearts of your faithful and enkindle in them the fire of your love."

DAY 4

When Mary and Joseph brought Jesus into the temple, Simeon, like a grandfather, took Jesus into his arms and blessed God by proclaiming that his eyes had now seen "salvation" (Luke 2:30). His words carry an even deeper meaning as we remember that the Hebrew name Jesus actually means "God saves." Simeon held salvation in his hands.

† During the 2020 COVID-19 pandemic, Pope Francis proclaimed, "Faith begins when we realize we are in need of salvation. We are not self-sufficient; by ourselves we flounder." Many of us have tried over and over again to conquer bad habits and destructive behaviors (called vices) by our own power. Where do you need salvation in your life? Ask the Holy Spirit today to help you in one specific area.

DAY 5

Simeon is not concerned with only his salvation; he is also concerned with the salvation of the Gentiles—that is, people who aren't Jewish. Jesus, the salvation of God, is proclaimed by Simeon to be "a light for revelation to the Gentiles" (Luke 2:32). Millennia before, God had promised that, through the patriarch Abraham, "all the families of the earth shall be blessed" (Genesis 12:3). God chose His people, Israel, and now, in Jesus Christ, this blessing is extended to all the nations, including you and me.

† Who in your life does not know Jesus or does not know Him well? Think about a way in which, with both gentleness and clarity, you might present Jesus, the light of revelation, to him or her.

DAY 6

We're only given a few details about Anna, but they're important. One is quite easy to miss: Anna is "of the tribe of Asher" (Luke 2:36), one of the 10 "lost tribes of Israel" who were conquered by the Assyrian Empire in 722 BC, their lineage lost to history. A few northern Israelites avoided the exile by escaping to the southern kingdom of Judah; Anna's ancestors must have been among them. Anna's presence as a daughter of the tribe of Asher shows God's care not only for the southern kingdom of Judah and for the Gentiles but even for the lost tribes who, because of their unfaithfulness, had been conquered.

† "If we are unfaithful, he remains faithful—for he cannot deny himself" (2 Timothy 2:13). The northern tribes were unfaithful, yet God continued to reach out to them. Thank God for one time in your life when He continued to reach out to you even when you were unfaithful to Him.

DAY 7

Anna was both a widow and a prophet who "did not depart from the temple, worshiping with fasting and prayer night and day" (Luke 2:37). In ancient Israel, there was a group of young women, temporarily consecrated virgins, who lived at the temple, praying and serving in various ways until it was their time to pursue marriage. Although we cannot be sure if Anna, a widow, was one of these women—perhaps looking after and instructing the girls—her total dedication to God for most of her life provides an example for us all of deep devotion to God.

† What is one thing you can do to deepen your devotion to God? Perhaps spend five minutes per day reading your Bible or do a little bit of fasting this week.

WEEK 7

St. Josephine Bakhita

Religious sister

Patron saint of Sudan, South Sudan, and victims of human trafficking

FEAST DAY: February 8

DAY 1

Born in 1869 in the small village of Olgossa in what is now Sudan on the continent of Africa, this future saint lived a happy and carefree life until, at seven or eight years old, she was captured by slave traders, forced to walk barefoot for around 600 miles and, over the course of 12 years, sold multiple times. Her captors gave her the name Bakhita, Arabic for "lucky"—a name that seemed like the exact opposite of her life at the time. In fact, she was so terribly abused that she forgot the name her parents had given her.

† What does your name mean? If you share your name with a saint, look that saint up and ask him or her to pray for you. If you don't share your name with a saint, find a saint with a common interest, perhaps by searching "patron saint of _____" online, and ask that saint to pray for you.

DAY 2

After being sold at least twice and suffering many abuses, Bakhita was purchased by an Italian vice consul named Callisto Legnani. In 1885, she left Sudan with him and arrived in Italy. While Legnani apparently had no qualms about buying another human being, he consistently treated her with kindness. Bakhita found this a surprising and welcome difference from her previous captors. This was the first time since her kidnapping that she did not have to fear she would receive a lashing.

† Of course, the relationship between two people is not the same as the relationship between a person and God, but it's worth remembering that sometimes we see God as someone ready to lash us rather than as someone ready to treat us kindly. Open your Bible today and read Isaiah 43:1–4, remembering how deeply your true Lord and Savior loves you.

DAY 3

Upon her arrival in Italy, Bakhita was given to the Michieli family to act as a nanny for their daughter, Mimmina. Again, although they didn't seem to have a problem with owning a person, they treated her with kindness. While the Michielis were traveling for business, they left Bakhita and Mimmina in the care of the Canossian Sisters of the Institute of the Catechumens in Venice. This would lead to Bakhita's eventual baptism as a Catholic and, later, to her consecration as a bride of Christ—a nun.

† Bakhita had no idea that the "coincidence" of being left with the sisters would literally change her life. But God used even the simple necessity of business travel to show her His love through these sisters. What is one way you can identify the Holy Spirit conspiring with the circumstances of your own life to show you His deep love?

DAY 4

With the sisters, Bakhita first came to know God, whom "she had experienced in her heart without knowing who He was." She wrote, "Seeing the sun, the moon and the stars, I said to myself: Who could be the Master of these beautiful things? And I felt a great desire to see him, to know Him and to pay Him homage." While she and Mimmina were with the Canossian Sisters, Bakhita entered the catechumenate, meaning she was preparing for baptism. After several months of preparation, she received the sacraments of baptism, confirmation, and Holy Communion on January 9, 1890. After this, she could often be found kissing the baptismal font and exclaiming, "Here, I became a daughter of God!"

✝ Have you been baptized? Thank God for the gift of your baptism today. If you live close by, make a short pilgrimage to the church where you were baptized this week and make Bakhita's thanksgiving at the baptismal font there.

DAY 5

This deep love for God was not just a one-time experience for Bakhita, who had now received the baptismal name Josephine. When the Michielis returned from their travels, Josephine asked if she could stay with the Canossian Sisters, devoting herself totally to the God with whom she had fallen in love. Josephine was freed from slavery to humans and entered into the free, sweet servitude of Jesus Christ. On December 8, 1896—the Solemnity of the Immaculate Conception of the Blessed Virgin Mary—Josephine Bakhita became a bride of Christ, consecrated to God, whom she would from then on call, with sweet devotion, "my Master."

✝ Open your Bible today. Read Isaiah 54:4-10 and think about the great love God has as He speaks those words directly to you.

DAY 6

Jesus Christ was a Master who had been flogged as Bakhita had, a Master who had come in compassion to meet His beloved, "lucky" Josephine. She'd tell anyone who would listen, "Be good, love the Lord, pray for those who do not know Him. What a great grace it is to know God!"

† God is not a distant Master or slave trader. God is our *Father*! Josephine wanted everyone to know this truth. Offer prayers today for those who don't know God. Pray for those who have not received the great gift of baptism. Ask God for them to be converted and live.

DAY 7

During her 50 years as a nun, Josephine did no extraordinary things. She simply did "ordinary things with extraordinary love," a teaching the later St. Teresa of Calcutta often expressed. She cooked, sewed, embroidered, answered the door, and was a simple witness of the love of God to everyone who crossed her path. Extraordinary forgiveness. Extraordinary freedom. Extraordinary love in each moment of her life. This is what made Josephine Bakhita a saint and truly "lucky."

† What if doing the "ordinary" things with faithfulness and love could make you a saint? Well, they can! What "ordinary" things does your vocation require of you? Like Josephine, do your ordinary duties with great love, and ask her to help you.

St. José Luis Sánchez del Río

Layperson and martyr

Patron saint of children, adolescents, and persecuted Christians

FEAST DAY: February 10

DAY 1

St. José Luis Sánchez del Río died a martyr on February 10, 1928, at just 14 years old. In 1926, after the Mexican Revolution, the Mexican government used provisions in the new constitution to legally begin a vast persecution of the Catholic Church, seizing properties, making priests state employees, requiring government approval of homilies, and banning religious garb. The popular uprising against this persecution would come to be known as the Cristero War, and St. José was one of its fighters.

† Even now, there remain places in the world where the practice of Christianity is illegal and where Christians can be killed for their faith in Jesus. What would you do if faced with the choice to deny Christ today?

DAY 2

In August 1926, the Cristero War began as rebels rose up against the oppression of the Mexican government. Their battle cry: "*¡Viva Cristo Rey!*" ("Long live Christ the King!"). At 14 years old, young José watched as his uncle, Father Ignacio, was shot in the leg by government representatives. José then joined the Cristeros in their battle for religious freedom in Mexico, working at various odd jobs to support the soldiers.

† One can disagree about whether or not José should have joined the rebellion, but it's hard to deny his great courage. Even if we're not in the midst of a war like José was, what can each of us do to defend Christ today? Maybe you can research places where there are persecuted Christians and do something to help. Maybe for you it's as simple as defending those who are defamed by gossip.

DAY 3

Unfortunately, young José was captured. His captors tried to get him to deny Christ. "Simply say, 'Death to Christ the King!'" they told him. But José would not. He only shouted the Cristeros' battle cry: "Long live Christ the King!"

† This reminds me of another important moment from the Bible. In John 19:15-16, the crowds cried out, "Away with [Jesus], away with him, crucify him!" Pilate asked them, "Shall I crucify your king?" and the chief priests replied, "We have no king but Caesar." But if they were observant Jews, they would have said, "We have no king but *God*." What are we as Christians making king in our lives? How can you truly accept Jesus more fully as King of your own life?

DAY 4

Imprisoned in a parish church that had been transformed into a prison, José prayed the rosary daily and wrote to his mother, expressing his willingness to die a martyr's death. Once, he was made to watch another Cristero being hanged. Instead of being cowed, José encouraged the man, reminding him that soon he would be with Jesus in heaven.

† We Christians are called to "encourage one another and build one another up" (1 Thessalonians 5:11). In the direst circumstances, José built his brother up in love. We each know people who are suffering. With a kind word or a simple gesture, we can encourage them in their journeys. Who—maybe at work, at school, or in your family—can you encourage today?

DAY 5

It would soon be José's time to be with Jesus in heaven as well. One night, he watched three roosters making a mess on the altar of the church. In zeal for the Lord's house, he wrung the necks of the three roosters, which turned out to belong to his godfather, who was also the town's mayor. Enraged and ignoring his duty to help José live the faith, his godfather did the opposite. He ordered José to be murdered that very night.

† Ask yourself: How reverent am I in church? Do I remember that I am in the presence of God? Do I remember that this building has been consecrated, set apart for the worship of God? This Sunday, come to church five minutes early to prepare your soul for Mass. Then stay five minutes late to thank Jesus. Treat it as a place of reverence; refrain from casually visiting inside the church.

DAY 6

Soldiers cut the soles of José's feet and made him walk to the cemetery where he was going to be buried, slashing at him with machetes as he walked. Despite his great pain and the soldiers' repeated requests that he deny the faith, young José would only proclaim, "Long live Christ the King!"

† Holy men and women of old would often use the phrase *Memento mori*, Latin for "Remember that you're going to die." They didn't say this out of morbidity, but rather as a reminder to live in such a way that if you died tomorrow, you would be confident standing before the throne of God. If we remember daily that we're going to die, we will live more joyously and courageously. Then, when it is time to die, we will be prepared, like José, to meet Jesus and enter into heaven.

DAY 7

Shot in the head at around 10:00 p.m. on February 10, 1928, young José died a martyr and went to heaven. The people of the town, immediately understanding the blessing of martyrdom, began to gather even the dirt onto which his blood had fallen to have as relics of this young new saint.

† From the very beginning, Christians have gravitated toward the relics of the saints. Why? Because God has worked through them. "God did extraordinary miracles by the hands of Paul, so that handkerchiefs or aprons were carried away from his body to the sick, and diseases left them and the evil spirits came out of them" (Acts 19:11–12). In the Old Testament, simply touching the bones of the prophet Elisha raised a man from the dead (2 Kings 13:21). May we be as devoted to God and as confident in His work through His saints.

St. Katharine Drexel

Religious sister and founder of the Sisters of the
Blessed Sacrament

Patron saint of philanthropy and racial justice

FEAST DAY: March 3

DAY 1

On October 1, 2000, Katharine Drexel became the second person
born in the United States to be canonized (after St. Elizabeth Ann
Seton, whom we met in week 3). Born in 1858 in Philadelphia,
Pennsylvania, Katharine learned at home the great love for the
poor that showed the world she was a saint. Three times a week,
every week, the Drexel family served the poor from their own
home. Those who needed help with rent or clothing or food would
come to the door of the Drexel home, where the family would care
for them.

† None of our families are flawless, but almost all of our families
have taught us at least one good thing. What virtues did you
learn in your family? What's one way you can practice one of
your "family virtues" today?

DAY 2

Our families have difficulties, and so did Katharine's. When she was only five weeks old, her mother died. Her father remarried, and, thanks be to God, Katharine's stepmother deeply loved the family. But when Katharine was in her 20s, her stepmother lost a three-year battle with cancer. Shortly thereafter, her father died, too. Her parents' deaths left Katharine with both profound grief and a very large inheritance, shared with her two sisters. Perhaps it was the combination of suffering and service that gave her a heart for the poor. And her inheritance was a great asset in being of service.

† Think of a suffering in your life from which God drew forth a great good—maybe a job you didn't get that led to a better opportunity or a sickness that drew you closer to Him. Thank God for that time of suffering today.

DAY 3

The death of Katharine's father in 1885 came only 20 years after the Civil War. African Americans remained in dire straits. At the same time—though for different reasons—the suffering of Indigenous Americans was also acute. Equipped with the love for the poor they had learned at home and a deep love for Jesus, Katharine and her two sisters decided to use their wealth to provide necessities and education for Indigenous and African Americans, building their first school in Santa Fe, New Mexico, in 1887.

† Katharine and her sisters provided practical help to those in need. Which one of the corporal or spiritual works of mercy could you practice today? Corporal works of mercy are feeding the hungry, giving drink to the thirsty, clothing the naked, sheltering the homeless, visiting the sick, visiting the prisoner, and burying the dead. Spiritual works of mercy are instructing the ignorant, counseling the doubtful, admonishing sinners, bearing wrongs patiently, forgiving offenses willingly, comforting the afflicted, and praying for the living and the dead.

DAY 4

From an early age, Katharine had wanted to live devoted to Jesus as a cloistered nun. But she wouldn't make that decision on her own. As a young lady, she had met Father James O'Connor (later the bishop of Omaha, Nebraska) while teaching summer school classes in Torresdale, Pennsylvania. He became her spiritual director, and when she expressed to him her desire for the cloister, he gently encouraged her to wait and pray. It's good that she did, because she would later receive guidance from the pope himself.

† You may not have a spiritual director, but who in your life can you go to for good spiritual advice? We all need a wise spiritual person (or persons) in our lives to help us see the will of God, especially when our perception is fogged by grief, sin, busyness, or just a dry season in life. Say a little prayer today asking Jesus to show you who these people are in your life. If there aren't any, ask Him to send you one.

DAY 5

Having begun to finance missions for Indigenous Americans, the Drexel sisters needed missionaries to proclaim the gospel to them by word and deed. When they traveled to Rome and met with Pope Leo XIII to make this request in January 1887, he suggested that Katharine herself become a missionary. After two years of discernment (prayerful consideration) and under the guidance of now–Bishop O'Connor, Katharine began the formal process of becoming a nun in May 1889. Perhaps Bishop O'Connor had always had a sense that Katharine was destined for an active—rather than cloistered—mission in service to Jesus, her Bridegroom.

† The obedient person takes seriously the words spoken to him or her, considers them carefully, then takes action. Katharine had not yet made a vow of obedience, but she *was* obedient. She took Pope Leo's words to heart, considered them for two years, then took action. Is there a place in your life where God might be calling you to this kind of obedience?

DAY 6

The order Katharine founded was called the Sisters of the Blessed Sacrament. She could have chosen just about any name, but she chose to focus on the Eucharist, which was the source of her love for the poor, the oppressed, and those under the oppression of racism. By means of their very name, Katharine's spiritual daughters are daily reminded of their great foundress's focus on what the later *Catechism of the Catholic Church* calls the "source and summit of the Christian life."

† Make a visit to your local parish church today to spend some time with Jesus in the Blessed Sacrament. While you're there, perhaps open your Bible and read John 6:22-71.

DAY 7

In 2011, Katharine Drexel was inducted into the National Women's Hall of Fame, joining fellow saints Elizabeth Ann Seton and Marianne Cope as women who are recognized for having made a significant impact on the United States of America. To be a saint in the model of Katharine Drexel is to be a true humanist, one who cares for the development of the whole human person. Honors like this one give a glimpse into the powerful positive impact saints have on human society.

† What's one way that you can have a positive impact on human society? Can you tutor children who struggle in school? Volunteer at the food bank? Produce art or music? Or—simplest but perhaps most difficult—can you love and serve your family with zealous devotion?

WEEK 10

St. Perpetua & St. Felicity

Martyrs

Patron saints of mothers, expectant mothers, butchers, ranchers, Catalonia, and the city of Carthage

FEAST DAY: March 7

DAY 1

In the year AD 203, in the ancient North African city of Carthage, five catechumens (people preparing to become Christians) were rounded up and thrown into a dungeon for their faith. One of them, Perpetua, was a 22-year-old noblewoman, married, and mother to an infant son. Her son wasn't there with her, which was a problem not only because she missed him but also because he hadn't yet been weaned. He would die if he weren't allowed to be with her. Perpetua begged and begged for her son to be kept with her in prison. When her captors relented and her son was brought to her, Perpetua wrote in her journal, "The dungeon became to me, as it were, a palace so that I preferred being there than to being elsewhere."

† What love Perpetua shows for her son! Ask Jesus today to increase your love for your family, then do one practical act of love for one of your family members, like washing the dishes even though it's not your turn.

DAY 2

Perpetua's brother, who was also among the prisoners, saw that she was favored by God, so he asked her to pray for a revelation about whether they would be martyred or freed. The Bible records that one of the 12 Apostles was also favored by God: John, who is called "the beloved disciple." At the Last Supper, Peter, the Prince of the Apostles, did almost the exact same thing Perpetua's brother did: "One of his disciples, whom Jesus loved, was lying close to the breast of Jesus; so Simon Peter beckoned to him and said, 'Tell us who it is of whom he speaks'" (John 13:23–24). Jesus revealed to John the identity of Judas the betrayer.

† Some of us, like John and Perpetua, receive greater favors from God. Some, like Peter, are given greater authority. Others, like the remaining Apostles, are given different gifts. Read 1 Corinthians 12:4–13:13 today, ask God to show you your gifts, and thank Him for them.

DAY 3

Encouraged by her brother, Perpetua prayed to know how their imprisonment would end. She received a vision, which she recorded in her journal, of a golden ladder stretching up to heaven, lined by "swords, lances, hooks, and knives," with a giant dragon at the bottom to discourage any climbers. Both she and a fellow prisoner named Saturus were able to climb the ladder without being hurt by the dragon or the weapons. At the top, they found a tall man with white hair in shepherd's clothes in the middle of an enormous garden. "He was milking his sheep, surrounded with many thousands of persons clad in white. He called me by my name, bid me welcome, and gave me some curds made of the milk which he had drawn: I put my hands together and took and ate them; and all that were present said aloud, Amen." From this vision, she concluded that she and the other prisoners would die as martyrs.

† What great surrender Perpetua had! Turn to page 213 and pray the words of the Surrender Novena all at once today.

DAY 4

Later, Perpetua's father, with good intentions and great affection, encouraged Perpetua to commit the mortal sin of idolatry by worshiping the emperor. But Perpetua was not willing to turn her back on God to save her own skin. Her father then appealed to her great human love for her family and her son, tempting her to deny her God. "Have pity my daughter, on my grey hairs. Have pity on your father, if I am worthy to be called a father by you . . . Have regard to your brothers, have regard to your mother and your aunt, have regard to your son, who will not be able to live after you. Lay aside your courage, and do not bring us all to destruction . . ."

† Often, the saints are misunderstood. While saints-in-the-making are thinking with the supernatural perspective of Jesus, people who love them are thinking from the perspective of this world. It is therefore very important that those of us who want to be saints (canonized or not) have wise, spiritual people in our lives from whom we can gain advice. Who is a wise, spiritual person in your life? Is there anything going on right now you'd like to consult him or her about?

DAY 5

Rather than succumb to these temptations, Perpetua commended her son to the care of the Lord. She prayed deeply for him, and even though he was very young, he no longer wanted or needed to nurse. Instead, he was able to begin eating solid food. Perpetua had been presented with the temptation to deny Jesus, supposedly for the sake of her son. She said, in essence, "No! I will trust Jesus." And Jesus provided, because He always provides what we need. That doesn't mean He always provides what we *want*. In fact, He often doesn't, because what we want often isn't what's best for us. But He always provides what we need.

† It is amazing—miraculous even—what Jesus will do when we place all of our trust in Him. Turn to page 210 and pray the Litany of Trust.

DAY 6

Perpetua went to her martyrdom because she trusted and she loved. Her mother-love was natural; her martyr-love was supernatural. By trusting in Jesus, she allowed Him to build on her natural mother-love. She allowed God to raise her up, to perfect her, so that she could give her life for Him.

† Right after Jesus told His disciples about His coming suffering and death, He took Peter, James, and John up the Mount of Transfiguration to open their eyes to the supernatural reality at hand. Today, pray with (i.e., read and reflect upon) Matthew 16:21–17:7. Ask Jesus for the grace to see His supernatural love in every aspect of your life.

DAY 7

Felicity, an enslaved woman who was imprisoned with Perpetua and the others, was eight months pregnant as the day of their martyrdom approached. She and the other prisoners prayed that she would give birth before that day. As soon as they finished praying, her labor began. As she cried out in the pains of childbirth, a soldier mocked her, asking what she would do when torn apart by wild beasts if she couldn't bear the pain of labor. Felicity answered, as recorded by Perpetua in her journal, "It is I that suffer what I now suffer; but then there will be another in me that will suffer for me, because I shall suffer for him." Having delivered the baby, a little girl, Felicity entrusted her to a Christian woman who raised her as her own. On March 7, 203, Felicity—along with Perpetua and the others—courageously endured her martyrdom and joined her beloved Jesus in heaven.

† Open your Bible today and meditate on Hebrews 12:1–3. The saints could endure and even desire martyrdom because their eyes were set on the great gift of being *like* Jesus and being *with* Jesus. Ask for this grace today.

St. Frances of Rome

Layperson

Patron saint of Benedictine oblates, automobile drivers, and widows

FEAST DAY: March 9

DAY 1

Frances of Rome was born in 1384 and died on March 9, 1440. She wanted to become a nun, but instead she followed her parents' wishes and married Lorenzo Ponziani, an extremely wealthy commander in the papal army, in 1396. In the midst of her great desire for religious life, not to mention her great devotion to and capacity for prayer, Frances was willing to leave her prayers for a time if called away by her husband or anyone else in her family who needed her. She thus lived by her own words: "A married woman must, when called upon, quit her devotions to God at the altar to find him in her household affairs."

✝ Pope St. John Paul II wrote that everyday Christians have a vocation—a special calling from God—to seek His Kingdom precisely by engaging in the daily things of life and, like Frances, doing them out of devotion to God and neighbor. Can you offer your grocery shopping, grass cutting, or bill paying to God? Say, "Jesus, I do these chores out of love for you and for my family. Please be with me in them and make me a saint."

DAY 2

One miraculous example of Frances's calling to daily care is that, after being called away from her prayers four times to care for others in the midst of praying one single Bible verse, Frances returned to find the verse written in gold letters.

† We all get distracted sometimes when we stop to pray. Good prayer doesn't depend on *not* getting distracted but on what we *do* with those distractions. The next time you find yourself distracted in prayer, imagine taking the person or thing that comes to mind and placing him/her/it into the hands of Jesus.

DAY 3

Frances also showed her devotion to her vocation as mistress of her household by treating her servants as brothers and sisters, zealously encouraging them to work for true and lasting happiness by living as disciples of our Lord Jesus Christ. Renowned for her care for the poor, Frances was similarly able to bring many upper-class Roman ladies into a life of deep devotion to Jesus. These ladies became associated with a Benedictine monastery in the city by becoming "oblates" of St. Benedict, devoting themselves to prayer and good works but without the formal vows of nuns.

† An "oblation" is an offering. An "oblate" is one who has offered herself or himself in service. Many religious orders have groups of oblates, also known as "third orders" or "tertiaries," in which laypeople offer themselves in service to God under the guidance of the Benedictines, Franciscans, Dominicans, or other orders. If this strikes you, read up on a few religious orders and ask Jesus if you should discern becoming an oblate.

DAY 4

In an age of political turbulence, Frances's husband, Lorenzo, was exiled from Rome, his property stolen, his house demolished, and his eldest son, Giovanni Battista, taken as a hostage. Frances stood by him in all these trials. Quoting the book of Job, she said, "God hath given, and God hath taken away. I rejoice in these losses, because they are God's will. Whatever he sends, I shall continually bless and praise his name for."

† Frances allowed her suffering to be an opportunity to grow closer to Jesus. May we always do the same. "For one is approved if, mindful of God, he endures pain while suffering unjustly . . . For to this you have been called, because Christ also suffered for you, leaving you an example, that you should follow in his steps" (1 Peter 2:19, 21).

DAY 5

Fortunately, Lorenzo was eventually able to return from exile and was given back his property. Lorenzo and Frances lived a holy married life together, praying, sacrificing, and fulfilling their duties to one another as happily married husband and wife. One spiritual practice they engaged in was "marital continence," or temporarily abstaining from sexual relations within marriage, which increased their love and devotion to God (see 1 Corinthians 7:1–7).

† In Matthew 19:12, Jesus praises those who have renounced marriage "for the sake of the kingdom of heaven." Similarly, St. Paul extols the virtues of not getting married (or of temporarily forgoing the marital embrace like Lorenzo and Frances) for the sake of "undivided devotion to the Lord" (1 Corinthians 7:35). Therefore, while marriage is good—very good (Genesis 1:26–28)—engaging in either permanent or periodic times of celibacy or continence is a holy thing, which, when done properly, increases devotion to God.

DAY 6

After Lorenzo's death in 1436, Frances devoted herself full time to prayer, penance, and good works for the remaining four years of her life. To facilitate this type of life, she joined the community of oblates she had founded as a regular member. After walking barefoot to the monastery, Frances lay facedown before the women who were her own spiritual children and begged to be allowed to enter.

† Frances's humility is striking. The word "humility" comes from the same root word as *humus*, Latin for "ground" or "dirt." This is also the root of the word "human." "You are dust, and to dust you shall return," says God to Adam and Eve (Genesis 3:19). To be a humble Christian means to remember, like Frances, that we are mere dust and, at the same time, deeply, intensely loved by God.

DAY 7

Deeply devoted to her spiritual exercise, Frances left it only to serve the poor. She became, as the *Catholic Encyclopedia* puts it, "one of the greatest mystics of the fifteenth century." In the midst of her prayer and penance, Frances was granted mystical visions and ecstasies. She was particularly moved with love of God at Mass, especially as she received Holy Communion. She also had frequent conversations with her guardian angel.

† Extraordinary mystical experiences like visions and physically manifested supernatural encounters are just that—extraordinary. Don't search for visions of angels. Instead, search the Scriptures and the liturgy for a relationship with the God whom the angels serve. There you'll find the heights of fulfillment and true happiness—and if you're granted visions of angels while you're there, thanks be to God!

WEEK 12

St. Patrick

Bishop, confessor, Apostle of Ireland

Patron saint of Ireland, engineers, paralegals, and those experiencing problems with snakes

FEAST DAY: March 17

DAY 1

Patrick was most likely born in the fifth century in the Roman province of Brittania (modern-day England and Wales). At 16 years of age, he and other members of his father's household were kidnapped into slavery—not unlike our 19th-century friend Josephine Bakhita—and brought to Ireland. Patrick's life under slavery was difficult. He tended livestock in the forest and mountains and was given little food or clothing in spite of the rain, snow, and ice. Most of the time, he was alone.

† Jesus saved us in the midst of rejection, mistreatment, insults, and even death. He comes to us in the midst of our great sufferings with an offer and an opportunity for great joy. God doesn't directly cause suffering, but He allows it so He can use it to draw us closer to Himself. Can you think of a time of suffering in your life that God ended up using to bless you? Thank God for that today.

DAY 2

Patrick had been baptized but hadn't truly lived as a Christian before his capture. But something happened to Patrick during his hungry, cold-ridden flock tending: He began to pray. He had nowhere else to go and no one else he could turn to, so he was moved to turn to God. Because he carried his cross with Jesus, even his bodily sufferings became a source of grace for him.

† Take a moment today to reflect on Patrick's words from his *Confessions*: "The faith grew in me, and the spirit was roused, so that, in a single day, I have said as many as a hundred prayers, and in the night nearly the same, so that whilst in the woods and on the mountain, even before the dawn, I was roused to prayer and felt no hurt from it, whether there was snow or ice or rain ... because the spirit was then fervent within me."

DAY 3

After Patrick had spent many months alone, praying and tending the cattle, God informed him of his great mission: preaching the gospel. Patrick was told in a dream that he was meant to return to Britain and that a ship was waiting to take him there. Like Joseph of old, Patrick went faithfully to his mission (see Matthew 2:13–15, 19–23). After traveling a long distance, Patrick found the ship as expected. But the sailors refused to give him passage back to Britain—probably because he couldn't pay them.

† Commenting on this scene, Father Alban Butler, the most famous chronicler of the lives of the saints, wrote, "Thus new trials ever await the servants of God." Patrick was sure that God had called him to go back to England, but he immediately met an obstacle that was impossible for him to overcome alone. How often does that happen to us? May we remain faithful like Patrick!

DAY 4

As Patrick began to return to the forest, praying as he walked, the sailors called him back and decided to take him on board anyway. After three days of sailing, they made land, then wandered through Scotland for 27 days, nearly starving. The sailors, realizing that Patrick was close to God, asked him to pray for help. Patrick responded by inviting them to pray to Jesus for help themselves, even though they were not Christians. They did, and on that same day, they found food. God provided sustenance for the rest of their journey.

† If you've picked up a book like this one, you might have a reputation among your friends and family for being close to God. How often do people ask you to pray for them? The next time someone asks you to pray *for* them, instead pray *with* them, right there in the moment.

DAY 5

Patrick returned to his parents' home with great joy. After a time there, he was gifted with visions from God entrusting him with the mission of converting Ireland to Christianity. Again, like St. Joseph, Patrick rose and went. But first he needed to prepare. He prayed, he studied, and eventually he was ordained deacon, priest, and bishop, despite some opposition. As Butler wrote, "He forsook his family, sold, as he says, his birthright and dignity, to serve strangers, and consecrated his soul to God, to carry his name to the end of the earth."

† Have you asked God about your mission lately? Make this prayer today: "Jesus, would you reveal clearly to me how I am called to serve you at this season in my life?" Maybe there are strangers in your community for you to serve. Maybe He is calling you to a new devotion to your everyday duties as a spouse, parent, child, or neighbor. Maybe, if you're currently single, He is calling you to a life of complete consecration to Himself.

DAY 6

When Patrick arrived in Ireland as bishop, one of his very first acts opened the floodgates of God's grace in the country. Soon after his arrival, he visited the person who had enslaved him, paying the price of his ransom, as the *Catholic Encyclopedia* notes, "in exchange for the servitude and cruelty endured at his hands," which spurred the former slave master to turn to God and thereby receive His blessings. Patrick began his Irish mission by following the command and example of Jesus. This is the true "miracle" of the saints. Yes, sometimes the sick are healed, the sight of the blind is restored, and the rest. But the real power is in deep prayer, deep suffering, and deep forgiveness.

† Open your Bible today. Read Matthew 5:38-48. Ask God for the grace to courageously forgive and to courageously love, like Jesus and His servant Patrick.

DAY 7

In Ireland, Patrick found both great success and great suffering in his preaching. He was often spoken against and sometimes even beaten. But he saved many souls by baptizing them. He ordained many priests, consecrated many virgins and widows, and established monasteries. He gave freely of what he had without discriminating between Christians and non-Christians in his charity. He refused many offers of wealth from grateful people, and is said (though probably inaccurately) to have banished all snakes from Ireland.

† Thank God for the priest or deacon who baptized you today. Say a prayer for him. Then say a second prayer thanking God for the many faithful nuns, monks, and consecrated virgins who serve us—the Church—today, by giving glory to God and helping us become saints ourselves.

St. Cyril of Jerusalem

Bishop, confessor, and Doctor of the Church

Cyril could be considered a patron saint of catechumens (those preparing to become Christians by baptism) and neophytes (newly baptized Christians)

FEAST DAY: March 18

DAY 1

Born around AD 315 near the city of Jerusalem, Cyril was ordained a priest by Maximus, bishop of that city, when he was around 30 years old. As priest, Cyril's main responsibilities were preaching and teaching. Every Sunday, he preached to faithful Christians. He also taught and prayed with catechumens.

† Who in your life taught you the faith? Your parents? Your grandparents? Particular priests or deacons? Teachers at school or at church? Say a prayer thanking God for them today. If they are still with us, drop them a thank-you note.

DAY 2

In those days, the process of becoming a Christian usually took about two years—years filled with learning and prayer. Catechumens received the gift of baptism after showing that they could live a moral life and keep to the faith handed on to us by Jesus through the Apostles. As Jesus Himself said, "Every one to whom much is given, of him will much be required" (Luke 12:48). For this reason, those who want to become Christians must be well prepared so that, having received much in the gift of baptism, they can live the holy life expected of them.

✝ Most of us were baptized as infants and thus did not go through a catechumenate period. If you had to spend the next two years growing in virtue like the catechumens of old, what would you do?

DAY 3

Toward the end of the year 350, Cyril succeeded Maximus as bishop of Jerusalem. Several months later, God provided a miraculous sign, which Cyril described in a letter to Emperor Constantius II. On the morning of May 7, an enormous cross of light appeared in the sky over Golgotha, the place of our Lord's crucifixion and resurrection. This cross of light was so large that it stretched as far as the Mount of Olives two miles away.

✝ While Golgotha was the site of an extraordinary occurrence, often, when God does something physically extraordinary, He uses it to draw our attention to what is actually extraordinary in our ordinary. In which ordinary events of your life can you see God's work?

DAY 4

The city's populace saw the cross of light and ran to the church in fear and in joy. Young and old, Christians and pagans, citizens and strangers—all acclaimed the lordship of Jesus Christ, who works miracles like this one. This sign lasted for several hours, visible to all with a brightness greater than the sun. In his letter, Cyril encourages Constantius (who did not believe in the full divinity of Jesus) to take this as a sign to confess Jesus as truly and fully God (and thus be a true Christian).

† Many of those who saw this miracle ultimately reverted to their former way of life. Unlike the Christian catechumens Cyril had mentored, they did not take the path of prayer and sacrifice required to continue as Christians. May the fire of our love for God never go out. May it always be fed with the oxygen of prayer and sacrifice. Are you praying every day? Are you fasting regularly? These are the practices that will keep the fire of God's love ablaze in your heart.

DAY 5

Many so-called Christians in Jerusalem, like the emperor, did not believe that Jesus was fully God. (This is called the "Arian crisis" after the heretical priest Arius who argued for this incorrect belief.) For opposing the Arians, Cyril was driven out of his home of Jerusalem twice, spending a total of 17 years in exile due to his defense of the one true Catholic faith.

† Most saints have stories of great suffering. We've seen many already on our journey together. These sufferings—kisses of Christ from the cross—make us saints if we bear them well, because we are with Jesus in them. Let us suffer well and become saints.

DAY 6

The first time Cyril was driven from Jerusalem, it was because he was falsely accused of misappropriating church funds. The second time, he was accused of being a semi-Arian heretic himself, although he was faithfully fighting against them.

† It is very easy for us to spread false rumors about others—to gossip. Sometimes what we share is false. Other times, what we share is true, but we share it with people who have no need to know it, which is the sin of detraction, and then it can be misunderstood and passed along as something false. If you struggle with the sin of gossip or detraction, ask Jesus for the grace to stop, then focus on saying at least one good thing about someone else every day.

DAY 7

Upon the ascension of Julian the Apostate as emperor of Rome, Cyril was able to return to Jerusalem. (Julian, though vehemently against the Church, wanted to turn people against the Church by appearing to relax restrictions, rather than with violence.) Later, Cyril was again exiled under the Arian emperor Valens in 367, but he was restored after about 11 years under the reign of Gratian. In 386, he went to meet the Lord at the age of 70.

† Julian was a wicked emperor. However, God used even Julian's own selfish desires to work good for Cyril's mission of preaching the gospel. As the Bible teaches, "in everything God works for good with those who love him, who are called according to his purpose" (Romans 8:28). Ask God today to help you see how He works good even in the difficulties of your life.

St. Joseph

Spouse of the Blessed Virgin Mary, adoptive father of Our Lord Jesus Christ, Terror of Demons

Patron saint of fathers, workers, the dying, and the Church

FEAST DAY: March 19 (Solemnity of St. Joseph, Spouse of the Blessed Virgin Mary) and May 1 (Memorial of St. Joseph the Worker)

DAY 1

We meet Joseph in the first chapter of the first book of the New Testament—the Gospel according to Matthew—where we learn two important things about him. First, he is descended from the great King David. Second, he is "the husband of Mary, of whom Jesus was born" (Matthew 1:16).

† One of my favorite movie scenes is in *The Lion King*, when Simba, the young lion protagonist, is full of doubt. His father, Mufasa, from the heavens, says, "Remember who you are! You are my son!" Simba is encouraged to take up his mission in the world. You and I often find ourselves ashamed, afraid, and frozen because we define ourselves by our worst moments. Do not be afraid! Remember that you're a child of God, who is King of the universe. Like St. Joseph, live your mission with courage!

DAY 2

In ancient Jewish culture—unlike in our culture—newlyweds waited some months between their wedding and moving in together. During this time, the husband prepared a home for his new bride and family, often building it himself. When the angel Gabriel appeared to Mary and she conceived the child Jesus, Mary and Joseph were in this phase of married life. They were truly married, but they were not yet living together, because Joseph was still preparing their family home.

† How can you prepare your home for your spouse, for your children, or for those to whom you are called to show hospitality? Ask St. Joseph to teach you how to love others in the day-to-day life of your home.

DAY 3

During this stage of their married life, Joseph learned that Mary was with child. The Bible doesn't tell us how he learned of her pregnancy or the details of his reaction to the news. It seems to me that the most likely scenario is actually the simplest: Mary told Joseph what happened. They were married, after all. And they were both clearly very good and very holy people. Would we really think that Mary would hide the fact that an *angel of God* had appeared to her from her *husband*?

† If you're married or discerning (prayerfully considering) marriage, how's your communication with your spouse or potential spouse? If you're single, how's your communication with Jesus? Carve out some quality time this week to spend with your spouse, your potential spouse, or Jesus.

DAY 4

When Mary told Joseph what had happened, it seems that, in humility, Joseph thought that God wanted to reserve Mary wholly for himself. Humbly, Joseph was willing to give up his hoped-for married life with Mary. But if he publicly divorced her, she might be accused of adultery and stoned to death. He wanted to protect her, and so, "being a just man and unwilling to put her to shame, [he] resolved to send her away quietly" (Matthew 1:19).

† Joseph put the will of God and the good of his wife before his own desires. What is one area in your life where you can put the good of others before your own desires? Make a concrete resolution to do that this week.

DAY 5

Just because Joseph was just, that doesn't mean he was perfect. He had it wrong. God actually did want Joseph to be married to Mary—in a special, virginal marriage. God actually did want Joseph to father Jesus, even though Jesus was conceived in Mary's womb by a miraculous act of God and not by normal human means. To reveal this to Joseph, God sent an angel—perhaps Gabriel again—to say, "Joseph, son of David, do not fear to take Mary your wife . . . She will bear a son, and you shall call his name Jesus" (Matthew 1:20–21).

† When I played football in high school, if I realized I'd messed up in the middle of a play, I'd want to slow down and figure it out. But I couldn't, because my teammates were depending on me. Our coach would always say, "If you mess up, mess up going full speed. If you play scared of messing up, you're going to mess up more." Be like Joseph. Live at "full speed" as a Christian disciple. Pray a lot, work hard, and be not afraid!

DAY 6

The angel revealing Jesus's name to Joseph is very important, because in ancient Jewish culture, it was a father's role to give a child his or her name, and naming a child was a sign of adoption. Joseph, in humble obedience to God, adopted Jesus, making Him heir to the kingship of David, which the Old Testament tells us was a requirement to be the Messiah of Israel. Some say that Mary was also a descendant of David, and this may be true. But the Bible doesn't clearly tell us that; the Holy Spirit wants us to see, among other things, the great dignity of adoption. Jesus became part of the family of King David by being adopted, and we become part of the family of Jesus, God Himself and King of the Universe, by being adopted into His family at our baptism.

† Thank God for the gift of baptism—when you were adopted by God. Say a prayer also for children who are adopted and for their parents.

DAY 7

There are no recorded words from Joseph to the angel, no dialogue like Mary had with Gabriel. Joseph simply "did as the angel of the Lord commanded him" (Matthew 1:24). Over and over again, Joseph simply did as God desired. The family needed to go to Bethlehem, so they went. Then, to flee from the wicked King Herod, they had to go to Egypt, so they went. Then, when it was time to return from Egypt, Joseph "rose and took the child and his mother, and went" (Matthew 2:21).

† Joseph didn't complain. He didn't argue. He didn't overanalyze. He simply followed the will of God as faithfully as he could in every situation. May you and I live with the simple courage of Joseph.

WEEK 15

St. Isidore

Bishop, confessor, and Doctor of the Church

Patron saint of the internet, computer users, computer technicians, computer programmers, and students

FEAST DAY: April 4

DAY 1

St. Isidore is most famous these days because he is the patron saint of those who use the internet. Why is a man who lived 1,400 years ago (from AD 560 to 663) patron saint of the internet? Here's why: Isidore took all the facts he could gather and compiled them into what many consider the first encyclopedia, called the *Etymologiae*. This book was 448 chapters long and divided into 20 separate volumes, much like an encyclopedia on the shelf of a modern library. For around 1,000 years, Isidore's *Etymologiae* was the place to go if you had to look up anything, as today we most often go to the internet.

† Say a prayer asking Isidore to be with you, praying for you, so that you might use well the great tool of the internet.

DAY 2

Born in 560, Isidore is a Spanish saint, one of the greatest from that country. As we have seen with some of our other friends in heaven, Isidore belonged to a saintly family. His two brothers, Leander and Fulgentius, both became bishops, and, along with his sister Florentina, each attained a place among God's holy ones.

† Being around great examples is the best way to learn the ways of holiness. Who in your life should you spend more time with as a good example? Who provides bad examples to avoid?

DAY 3

Succeeding his brother Leander as bishop of the diocese of Seville, Isidore worked diligently to address the problems of the Christian community of his day. Since the time of Judas Iscariot and the fickle crowds in Jerusalem, the Church has never lacked in strife and difficulties. To remedy them, Isidore called or presided at three local synods, at which the region's bishops gathered to dialogue, debate, and decide on solutions to the problems plaguing Christians.

† It seems increasingly difficult these days to gather with people who disagree with us and civilly find solutions. The next time you find yourself in a disagreement, try to see the other person's point of view. Listen to them and respect them, even if you don't come to a consensus.

DAY 4

Although not a monk himself, Isidore recognized the great value of monastic life. He realized that to give one's life entirely over to prayer in deep, spousal relationship with God, as monks and nuns do, is the highest possible calling. As bishop, he designated himself protector of the monks, guarding them so they could remain entirely devoted to their life of complete and uninterrupted focus on the Lord.

† We may not be called to be monks or nuns, but even in the activity of our daily duties, we are called to remember Jesus and sit at His feet. Read Luke 10:38-42 today and ask Jesus to help you remember that He is the one thing necessary.

DAY 5

Isidore lived to be almost 80 years old, continuing in prayer and good works until the very end. During the last six months of his life, poor people came from far and wide to his doorstep to beg for help. His care for them was so great that his last act before death was to forgive the debts of everyone who owed him money and to ask that all of his remaining money be distributed to the poor.

† As Christians, we have a duty to serve the poor. Open your Bible and read Matthew 25:31-46. Then choose one concrete way to serve the poor this week and do it.

DAY 6

Just before giving away all his possessions, Isidore called two bishops to him so that he could be forgiven of his sins prior to his death. In doing so, he was following the explicit teaching of the Letter of James in the Bible: "Is anyone sick among you? Let him call the priests of the church and let them pray for him, anointing him with oil in the name of the Lord. And the prayer of faith will save the sick person and the Lord will raise him up. And if he has committed sins, they will be forgiven him" (James 5:14–15, author's translation).

† We can all call on priests to pray for us. Of course, if you or someone you love is in danger of death, call your priest so he can pray, anoint, and provide forgiveness from God for you or your loved one. But, hoping that you won't need to do so anytime soon, think of something you could ask your priest to pray for this week, then ask him the next time you see him.

DAY 7

Four days before he died, Isidore also asked the two bishops to provide Holy Communion for him. The Church puts a very high value on receiving the Eucharist (which is the body, blood, soul, and divinity of our Lord Jesus Christ) shortly before death. This final Eucharist is called *viaticum*—literally in Latin, "with you [on] the way." We receive our Blessed Lord, asking for the strength to persevere through our final struggle: letting go of this earthly life. With our sins forgiven through anointing and confession, we pass into the arms of God our Father.

† With modern medical technology like intubation and narcotic pain medication, many people can't receive even the smallest particle of the Sacred Host as they enter into the time immediately prior to death. If someone you love is dying, think about how it may be possible for them to have viaticum. Call your priest early so that your loved one can receive this great gift of our Lord Jesus Christ Himself.

St. George

Martyr

Patron saint of soldiers, scouts, and those engaging in military-style activities such as archery and equestrianism

FEAST DAY: April 23

DAY 1

St. George is one of the most popular saints in the history of Christianity. Among Greek Christians, he is called the Great Martyr, and even today, his statue stands a short distance away from the birthplace of Jesus in Bethlehem, although he lived almost three centuries later. It's said that Emperor Constantine the Great, a contemporary of George, built the first church dedicated to his patronage.

† George may have been known during his lifetime—he was, after all, a Roman official—but his popularity didn't explode until after his martyrdom. If we simply do the duties of our lives while praying, fasting, and giving to the poor, we too will become saints. Let us follow the example of George, searching for holiness over popularity.

DAY 2

George, like our friends Basil and Gregory, was raised by
Christian parents in the region of modern-day Turkey called
Cappadocia. However, he seems to have been born in the city of
Lydda (now known as Lod) in what is now Israel. His father died
early, perhaps while serving in the Roman army, and his mother
moved the family back near Lydda, where she had grown up and
still owned property.

† George is one of the precious few saints after the time of
Jesus to hail from the Holy Land, a region ravaged by strife,
war, and persecution. Pray today for the people in the Holy
Land and surrounding areas.

DAY 3

George became a soldier in the Roman army and quickly rose to
the rank of tribune, which is roughly equivalent to the modern
rank of colonel. He seems to have become so well respected that
he spoke with Emperor Diocletian himself. Diocletian, however,
eventually chose to begin persecuting Christians, blaming them
for problems in the empire.

† The profession of a soldier is a noble one. But many of our
soldiers, having given themselves to serve us by protecting
us, find themselves suffering from addictions, homelessness,
and post-traumatic stress. Pray a decade of the rosary today
for our soldiers and our veterans, asking George to pray with
you. If you feel so inclined, look up practical ways to help
them with your time or money.

DAY 4

George, a fervent Christian, courageously stood up to Emperor Diocletian, calling him out for the murder of Christians. In those days, edicts—public commands from the emperor—were written on paper and nailed to walls in the city for the public to see. Some say that George tore down these unjust edicts himself. As a reward for his courage, George was blessed with the crown of martyrdom. Diocletian had him thrown into prison and tortured, all the while tempting him to renounce Christianity. George, with the courage of a soldier, withstood these persecutions. Keeping the faith, he was beheaded and entered into heaven on April 23, 303.

† Although most of us are not in danger of being martyrs, we're each faced with choices either to stand up courageously for Jesus in our world or to remain silent while Jesus is disrespected and unloved. What is one way in your daily life that you can be courageous like George? Ask him to help you.

DAY 5

George is probably most famous for the tale of his battle with the dragon plaguing the city of Cyrene in Libya. While this story, found in Jacob of Voragine's 13th-century *Golden Legend*, is probably fictitious, it helps us see George's virtues and the eventual virtues of the people of Cyrene—virtues we should imitate if we want to become saints.

† What kind of fiction do you consume? Books, movies, TV shows? Does the fiction you consume move you toward goodness, virtue, and saintliness? Or does it drag you down? Evaluate your fiction consumption today and begin reading and watching only things that build you up.

DAY 6

In the tale of St. George and the dragon, George was passing through Cyrene, whose inhabitants were forced to offer first sheep, then humans in sacrifice to the beast. George asked the princess of the region, Sabra, what was happening. Sabra, who was next to be sacrificed, told George about the dragon and begged him to leave before it devoured him, too. Just then, the dragon arrived. George immediately made the sign of the cross upon himself and his horse. By the power of the cross, George tamed and then slew the dragon, to the amazement of the people of Cyrene, who were then baptized into Christ.

† The common image of St. George slaying the dragon is meant to show you and me—called to be saints like George—how to use faith and courage to conquer the devil (called the "great dragon" in Revelation 12:9). Whenever you're tempted to sin, make the sign of the cross with devotion and say—out loud if you can—the name of Jesus.

DAY 7

George is the patron saint of those in the military because of both his profession as a soldier and his miraculous heavenly intercession for other soldiers after his death. During the first crusade, the French knights, tired and hungry, were given hope and strength when George appeared to them before the Battle of Antioch in 1098. They won. The following year, George is said to have appeared to King Richard the Lionhearted just prior to the siege of Jerusalem. Richard told his troops of this apparition, and, emboldened by their assurance of heavenly help, their siege was successful.

† Although apparitions are exceptional, the example of the saints is always here to encourage us. Which saint have you most identified with so far in this book? Do a little more research on that saint. Write down some points of his or her story that are particularly encouraging to you.

WEEK 17

St. Mark

Evangelist

Patron saint of Alexandria, Egypt; Venice, Italy; and barristers (a type of lawyer)

FEAST DAY: April 25

DAY 1

Mark was probably a Jew—descended from Aaron, brother of Moses—from Cyrene, the city where George is said later to have slayed the dragon. While scholars are divided on the details, most think that Mark was in Jerusalem at the time of the resurrection of Jesus. He may have been a disciple already (even one of the 70 sent out in Luke 10:1–17), or perhaps he was converted by the preaching of Peter. He may even have been one of the 3,000 baptized on that first Pentecost Sunday recorded in Acts 2.

† It is amazing how little we know about the past lives of some of our friends in heaven! Perhaps that is because their past is not as important as their present pointing us to Jesus. If your past was bad, make a better future with Jesus. And if your past was good, make a better future with Jesus.

DAY 2

Regardless of how Mark came to know Jesus, his zeal and hospitality (apparently shared with his mother) quickly served the building up of the Church. When Peter was rescued from prison by an angel, he found his way to Mark's mother's house, where the Christians had gathered together to pray. Later, Mark accompanied Paul and Barnabas on their journeys to preach the gospel of Jesus around the known world. He eventually ended up in Rome with Peter, who mentions him in 1 Peter 5:13.

† What does your zeal for the gospel look like? Write down three ways in which you're sharing the freedom and love of Jesus with others. If you can't think of three ways, resolve to begin.

DAY 3

Mark was zealous enough to follow the Lord wherever He led—except once. On one occasion, while on a missionary journey with Paul and Barnabas, he turned back, leaving them to return to his home in Jerusalem (Acts 13:13). The Bible doesn't tell us why, only that Paul saw Mark's turning back negatively (Acts 15:38).

† Are there times when you have turned back? Are you ashamed of those times? Ask Mark to help you. If you were in the wrong, ask forgiveness. Whether you were in the wrong or in the right, get back up. Start again. The past is gone. Live as a disciple of Jesus now.

DAY 4

Mark then began journeying with Barnabas and eventually found himself in Rome assisting Peter. Mark's Gospel is most likely St. Peter's preaching in written form. It's said that the Roman people asked him to write it down for them, and that Peter read, edited, and approved this Gospel. If Mark was a Jew from Cyrene, from a family wealthy enough to own a house in Jerusalem, it's likely that he would have been able to write easily in Greek and perhaps even to understand Latin, the language in which Peter may have preached in Rome. This allowed him to connect better with others and thereby to spread the gospel farther.

† There are many older and wiser people in our circles from whom we can learn. Find one of those people in your circles and sit down with them to gain wisdom, maybe over a cup of coffee. You might ask questions like these: What was it like growing up? What's something your mom or dad always said? What's your best advice as a parent?

DAY 5

Later, it is said, Peter sent missionaries from Rome to found other churches and charged Mark to serve as bishop of Alexandria in northern Egypt, the second greatest city of the world at the time. If Mark was originally from Cyrene, which was also in North Africa in the present-day country of Libya, this mission would have made lots of sense for him. Mark sailed from Rome to Cyrene. He preached all around North Africa for 12 years, performing many miracles, winning many converts to Christianity, and demolishing the worship of idols in many places.

† What gifts come from your heritage? Your family? Your culture? What is one way in which you could use these gifts from your home to tell other people about Jesus?

DAY 6

At the end of these 12 years, Mark was prompted by God to proceed to Alexandria, where many were converted very quickly. Such a vibrant church sprang up there that even Philo, the famous Jewish philosopher living in the city, took notice, describing the life of the local Christians. As we have seen in the lives of other holy bishops, such as Cyril of Jerusalem, Mark was persecuted. In fact, he was exiled from the city by non-Christians who were angered by the Holy Spirit's conversion of so many of their countrymen through his words and work. Accused of being a magician because of the miracles God worked through him, Mark was hunted by his enemies and eventually found while celebrating Mass.

† Envy is a powerful force for evil. If I'm envious, I am saddened at the good of others. I cannot handle others having success, or more success than me. Turn to page 217 and pray the Litany of Humility today.

DAY 7

Mark was seized, tied with cords, and dragged by an ox through the city streets. Although he was brutally tortured, bloodied, and battered, with pieces of his flesh torn off onto the rocks of the streets, Mark continued to praise God in his agony. His captors threw him into prison for the night, where he was comforted by two visions from God. The next day, April 25, 68, his captors dragged him again through town, where he eventually died. Christians gathered the remains of his maimed body and reverently buried him. Eventually, his body was moved to Alexandria and, later, in 815, to Venice (which explains why he is patron saint of Venice).

† Read Luke 22:29–46 today. Pay special attention to verse 43 and ask God for the grace to remain faithful when you suffer. Pray that God might always provide someone or something to give you the comfort you need to persevere in your sufferings.

St. Catherine of Siena

Virgin and Doctor of the Church

Patron saint of nurses, the ill, those who have suffered miscarriage, those who are ridiculed for their faith, and those who are tempted to sin

FEAST DAY: April 29

DAY 1

Catherine, the 23rd of 25 children, first received mystical visions at the age of five or six, when she saw Christ the King seated in glory, along with St. Peter, St. Paul, and St. John. At the age of seven, Catherine consecrated her whole life to God. She was so joyful that her family gave her the nickname "Euphrosyne," which is Greek for "joy."

✝ What holy things bring joy to your life? Do one of these things today.

DAY 2

When Catherine was 12, her parents worked to arrange a future marriage for her, but Catherine, conscious of the exclusive, spousal love of Jesus, refused. Her parents didn't listen to her, but Catherine redoubled her prayers and penances, depending on God to fulfill her desire to be totally His, and her parents relented—temporarily. About four years later, when 16-year-old Catherine's older sister died in childbirth, they encouraged her to marry her sister's widower. Catherine, of course, was completely opposed. She remained firm in her resolution to be exclusively for Jesus, and her parents eventually accepted that.

† Are you resolved to live a virtuous life? To avoid sin? To love your neighbor at every opportunity? Ask God for the gift of courage and resolve, like Catherine.

DAY 3

How did Catherine keep her resolve even in the midst of many trials? Let us listen to Catherine in her *Treatise of God's Providence* (quoted by Father Alban Butler and written in the third person): "That our Lord had taught her to build in her soul a private closet, strongly vaulted with the divine providence, and to keep herself always close and retired there; he assured her that by this means she should find peace and perpetual rest in her soul, which no storm or tribulation could disturb or interrupt."

† Catherine took time in silence and solitude to build this "private closet," which was kept secure by her trust in God's care for her. That's what "divine providence" means: God himself is ordering the universe and our lives. Often we think that the God who made the universe either isn't powerful enough or doesn't care enough to take care of us. Open your Bible to Isaiah 43:1-7 today and read the truth.

DAY 4

In the midst of her trials, from the "private closet" of her soul, Catherine sought to treat her parents and brothers with the dignity, honor, and respect they deserved. To achieve the needed mindset, she imagined her father in the place of Jesus, her mother in the place of Mary, and her brothers in the place of the Apostles. Because of her deep union with Jesus and her willingness to see her parents and siblings with their true dignity, she was able to humbly love, respect, and serve them, even as they placed obstacles in the path of her vocation of marriage to Jesus.

† It is all too easy to hate our enemies—and, yes, even beloved members of our families can be enemies to us at particular times. But Catherine chose something different. She used her imagination to help her choose love over hatred, respect over dishonor, and service over selfishness, even when the others were wrong. Use your imagination to help you see the true dignity of others, especially when they're wrong, and love them like Catherine.

DAY 5

At either 18 or 20 years of age, Catherine became a "third-order" Dominican (much like Frances of Rome had become a Benedictine oblate). She was not a nun. Instead, she was much more like a modern-day consecrated virgin. Deeply in love with God, Catherine desired to spend all of her time with Him, and for three years she lived in nearly complete silence and solitude. She spent her days in prayer, penance, and service to the poor, using her family's wealth to provide them with food and clothing.

† Most of us in contemporary society are driven to "do, do, do," "go, go, go," and to do it all *immediately*! But this was not how God led Catherine. He first led her to "be, be, be" with Him. Do you take time to build your "private closet" by being in solitude with Jesus? Find time every day to be alone with Jesus.

DAY 6

After those three years, Catherine emerged from her cell ready to work. Her solitude had emboldened her with deep healing and intimacy that freed her to live in apostolic boldness. As the *Catholic Encyclopedia* notes, she wrote "letters to men and women in every condition of life, entered into correspondence with the princes and republics of Italy, was consulted by the papal legates about the affairs of the Church, and set herself to heal the wounds of her native land by staying the fury of civil war and the ravages of faction." She even wrote to Pope Gregory XI to help convince him to return the papal court from Avignon to Rome.

†   Deep prayer always leads to deep love for God and neighbor.

DAY 7

Having accomplished many lifetimes' worth of work in 10 or 12 years of active ministry, Catherine died on April 29, 380, at the age of 33. The pope had returned to Rome from Avignon because of Catherine. Greater peace was attained in Italy because of Catherine. Many poor men and women were clothed and fed because of Catherine. And many other great things were accomplished through her. Catherine was possibly the most influential human being in the world for these 10 years of her life, all because she listened to Jesus, remaining always in communion with Him. Although she was neither pope nor bishop, much of the weight of the Church was laid on her shoulders, and she bore it well with His strength as one of the most courageous and influential Catholics of all time.

†   May we, like Catherine, always put God first, allowing our "doing" to come forth from our "being" with Him. Read Luke 10:38–42, remembering the example of Catherine as you read.

WEEK 19

St. Athanasius

Bishop, confessor, and Doctor of the Church

Athanasius could be considered a patron saint of theologians and those persecuted for defending the faith

FEAST DAY: May 2

DAY 1

Athanasius was born in AD 296 in Alexandria, Egypt. He would spend most of his life in his hometown, becoming bishop of the city and eventually dying there in the year 373. Unlike Catherine, who became very wise without any formal education, Athanasius became wise through the best of educations. He was blessed to study under St. Alexander, who would later precede him as bishop.

† Some of us are blessed, like Athanasius, to spend our whole lives in our hometowns. Others of us find ourselves far from home. Some could happily move home tomorrow, and others have said good riddance. But all of us have received growth and blessings from our hometowns. What is one of the blessings that the people of your hometown gave to you?

DAY 2

In his preaching and writing, Athanasius quoted the Bible so many times and with seemingly so much ease that it seems like he had the whole thing memorized. He had definitely filled his mind and heart with the Word of God by constantly immersing himself in it. But how did he know the *meaning* of the Scriptures? Athanasius wrote that he allowed the tradition of the Church to guide him, focusing particularly on the interpretations of the saints and martyrs who had come before him.

† Do you love the Bible? Do you read it (or listen to it) daily? Spend five minutes reading one of the Gospels today. If you don't have a Bible on hand, you can download a Bible app on your phone. There are even apps which have both the text and audio of the Bible for free.

DAY 3

Shortly after Alexander, his former teacher, was made bishop of Alexandria, around AD 313, Athanasius journeyed to the desert, where he spent a couple of years with St. Anthony (whom we met earlier in this book) in preparation for receiving the sacrament of Holy Orders. After he returned from the desert, Athanasius continued his formation, fulfilled many roles in the Church, and was ordained a deacon in 319. Alexander, his former tutor and now bishop, began to lean heavily on his advice.

† Many of the saints, like Athanasius and Catherine, had monumental impacts on world history. And almost all of them—from the Apostles, who spent three years in formation living with Jesus, down through present-day saints—have taken significant time in some kind of retreat. For Catherine, it was in her room, and for Athanasius, it was in the desert. Try to go on a weekend retreat sometime soon. Ask around your parish or contact your pastor to see if any are coming up.

DAY 4

There was a priest in the city of Alexandria named Arius, who was jealous of Alexander for becoming bishop of the city. In his pride and resentment, Arius began to assert that Jesus was not truly God, which is, of course, incorrect. This false teaching spread widely, causing such trouble that in AD 325, the emperor himself asked all of the world's bishops to gather in the city of Nicaea to resolve the question. Bishop Alexander took Athanasius the deacon with him to this ecumenical council, where Athanasius showed himself both wise and holy by defending the truth of the Bible and Christian tradition.

✝   Athanasius offered a great service to God's people while still a deacon. Does your parish have a deacon? Or do you know any deacons? Thank God for them today, and if you can, write a note to a deacon or two, thanking them for their ministry.

DAY 5

Athanasius's great knowledge of both the Bible and tradition was absolutely critical for his work as a deacon and, later, as bishop of Alexandria (which he became after Alexander died in 326). Arius and his followers would falsely say that "there was a time when the Son was not," even trying to cite the Greek translation of Proverbs 8:22 to support their position. Athanasius, however, knew how to interpret both the book of Proverbs and the rest of the Bible, because he had learned it in the context of the tradition of the Church, which the Bible says is "the pillar and bulwark of the truth" (1 Timothy 3:15). He knew that, in truth, Jesus is both "my Lord and my God" (John 20:28).

✝   How do you stay plugged in to the teaching of the Church? You could begin reading the *Catechism of the Catholic Church* or look into praying the Liturgy of the Hours (the Breviary), which is the official set of prayers marking the hours of each day and sanctifying the day with prayer.

DAY 6

During most of his 46 years as bishop of Alexandria, Athanasius was falsely accused by his Arian enemies. On one occasion, he was accused of murder and ordered to trial by Emperor Constantine himself. Athanasius found himself on trial before fellow bishops who falsely accused him of sacrilege, adultery, murder, and magic. Although he was cleared of all charges, he was forbidden to return to Alexandria, where he had grown up and was bishop. Athanasius was so hated by the Arian bishops that he was later accused of causing riots, committing more murder, and stealing grain given by Constantine to the poor. And this only scratches the surface of the hatred, violence, and persecution leveled at our friend Athanasius.

✝ For much of Athanasius's life, it must have seemed like everyone was against him. Does it sometimes seem that way in your life? Keep to the truth. Don't stop doing good. Ask Athanasius to pray for you, and follow his example.

DAY 7

St. Gregory of Nazianzus, whom we met in week 2, called Athanasius a "true pillar of the church," saying that he was humble, courteous, "meek, gentle, compassionate, amiable in his discourse, but much more so in his life" and had such "an angelical disposition . . . that his reproof spoke the kindness of a father, and his commendation the authority of a master; and neither was his indulgence over tender, nor his severity harsh."

✝ Pick one of these virtues of Athanasius and put it into practice this week. For example, if you choose to be courteous, you could go out of your way to say please and thank you, let people cut in front of you in line, or hold doors for people walking behind you.

WEEK 20

St. Matthias

Apostle

Patron saint of alcoholics, carpenters, tailors, those who need hope, those who need perseverance, and those who suffer from smallpox

FEAST DAY: May 14

DAY 1

St. Matthias is the last of the 12 Apostles. The Bible tells us that after the betrayal of Judas and the Ascension of our Lord, Peter stood up among the now 120 disciples and, inspired by the Holy Spirit, proclaimed that another should take Judas's place. The Holy Spirit worked through Peter to choose Matthias, even though He had not yet descended upon the disciples at Pentecost. In the Old Testament, we see the Spirit coming upon certain people or groups in a temporary way like this. As Jesus Himself says, "The wind blows where it wills, and you hear the sound of it, but you do not know where it comes from or where it goes; so it is with every one who is born of the Spirit" (John 3:8).

✝ Although we know that the Spirit comes upon us in a permanent, irrevocable way at baptism and confirmation (John 3:5, Acts 8:14–17), we must not forget that God sometimes freely chooses to work outside of the normal course of things.

DAY 2

The man who was to become the 12th Apostle had to have been with the community of Christian disciples from the beginning and able to give witness to the resurrection of Jesus. The Church put forward two men who met these qualifications and were judged worthy of being leaders in the mission of the Church. Then, praying to God for guidance, they cast lots (kind of like modern-day dice) for the final decision. This is a beautiful example of how human reason (which is a gift from God), trust in God, and divine providence work together.

† If you have a decision to make today, follow the Apostles' model: think about it, pray for guidance, and leave the final result up to God.

DAY 3

This is the last we hear of Matthias in the Bible. Apparently, he went off quietly and faithfully to accomplish the mission now entrusted to him by Jesus through His Church led by Peter. I am reminded of our friend St. Joseph, who is a main character in only a couple of chapters in the Bible yet is one of the most important figures in the whole history of our salvation. Matthias, like Joseph, speaks no words recorded in the Bible. But as an Apostle of our Lord Jesus Christ, he faithfully and effectively fulfills the ministry given to him by God.

† Pray today for humility like Matthias and Joseph. Turn to page 217 and pray the Litany of Humility today.

DAY 4

We learn more about the life of Matthias from later writers of history, including St. Clement of Alexandria, Eusebius of Caesarea, and St. Jerome. These writers tell us that Matthias was numbered among the 70 (or 72) whom Jesus had sent out, two by two, "into every town and place where he himself was about to come" to proclaim the Kingdom of God (Luke 10:1–12). This teaches us two important lessons. First, we can't do this alone. Second, Jesus has *entrusted* you and me with the mission of preparing the way before Him.

† How are you preparing the way for the Lord? And who's helping you?

DAY 5

Each baptized Christian has what are called "charisms," or spiritual gifts. All of us, obviously, are called to a life of virtue and holiness (in a word, sainthood). But our particular gifts show in a special way the "many-sided wisdom of God" (Ephesians 3:10, author's translation). Clement teaches us that Matthias had a particular charism for mortification (offering sacrifices for Jesus). He was especially able to do penances such as fasting, which brought him closer to Christ, who fasted in the desert, was beaten and scourged, carried His cross, and suffered the horrible death of crucifixion. "If any man would come after me, let him deny himself and take up his cross daily and follow me" (Luke 9:23).

† Paul had charisms of learning and preaching, Nathaniel integrity, John faithfulness, and Matthias mortification. What are your personal charisms? How can you use them to help others? (Check out Sherry Weddell's *Forming Intentional Disciples* for more on this.)

DAY 6

Matthias brought the faith to Cappadocia (what is now central Turkey) and along the Caspian Sea to the east. We've already met three saints who spent some of their childhoods in Cappadocia—Basil, Gregory, and George, all of whom lived more than 200 years after Matthias—and there are many more whom we haven't met. The seeds Matthias sowed sprouted great fruit.

† How are you sowing seeds of the gospel? They don't have to be big seeds. It doesn't have to be acres and acres of farmland. You might not even see the results. But take courage and don't give up! Use your personal charisms to sow the seeds of the gospel.

DAY 7

Matthias was martyred in Colchis (pronounced KOLL-kis), along the coast of the Black Sea, probably with a halberd (a spear with an ax-head near the point), which is why he's often depicted with one in art. The martyrs are almost always depicted with the method of their torture and execution. Why? For the same reason we use images of the cross, one of the most painful methods of execution in the history of the world. The world and the devil made every attack against the saintly martyr, and he or she did not fail. The martyr has *conquered* the world, the flesh, and Satan himself by the power of the cross. The weapon Satan and the world brought against her or him was turned back on itself and became the weapon by which the martyr conquered.

† Thank God for your sufferings. Thank God for your temptations. And beg for the grace to bear them like Jesus and like His martyrs.

St. Rita of Cascia

Holy woman and religious sister

Patron saint of seemingly impossible causes, those who suffer marital problems, victims of spousal abuse, and mothers

FEAST DAY: May 22

DAY 1

Although married at around the age of 12 in an arrangement made by her parents (a common practice at the time), Rita chose to be like Jesus in truly caring for the soul of her husband. For 18 years, she lived in Cascia, Italy, as a model wife and mother. Rita's husband was cruel, immoral, and violent, and she patiently encouraged him to change his ways. As he stubbornly refused, Rita's heart was grieved to watch her twin sons fall into the same violent ways as their father. Her grief was turned to prayer as she united her tears with the tears of Jesus in His agony through unceasing prayer.

† Carry a small crucifix in your pocket. When you suffer, grab that crucifix and suffer with Jesus like Rita.

DAY 2

Eventually, her husband was converted. He begged her forgiveness—which she freely gave—for the way he had treated her. Shortly afterward, he was murdered. Even as Rita grieved, she publicly forgave those who had killed him. Unfortunately, her grief was compounded as she learned that her sons had sworn a vendetta against their father's killer. She prayed that they would be prevented from carrying out their revenge. It would be better for them to die than to commit murder—and, sadly, they did. They both became ill, and as their mother tenderly cared for them, they too were converted and died, having both given and received forgiveness.

† Sometimes we think that the worst thing that can happen is physical death. But Rita knew that to be false. She knew that the worst thing is the spiritual, eternal death that mortal sin brings. Let's ask God today for the grace to see our sins like He does and to avoid mortal sin at all costs.

DAY 3

Rita, now 30 years old and without any family responsibilities, sought to become a nun. At that time, the Augustinian Convent in Cascia only allowed virgins to become nuns—ironic since the patron of the monastery was St. Mary Magdalene, whom Pope St. Gregory the Great tells us might even have been a prostitute prior to her encounter with Jesus and life of total dedication to Him in celibate chastity thereafter. If Mary Magdalene could be so exclusively dedicated to the Lord and patron of this convent, surely Rita the widow, who had been amazingly virtuous for her entire life, could be admitted.

† Jesus commands us to be perfect (Matthew 5:48). He does not command us to *have been* perfect. Rita had lived an amazingly holy and virtuous life. Mary Magdalene had not. But they were both chosen for deep, abiding, exclusive relationships with Jesus. Don't let the sins of your past undermine the holiness of your future.

DAY 4

Three times Rita asked to be admitted, and three times the prioress reluctantly refused, since the nuns' constitution forbade it. But after much prayer and waiting, the rules were relaxed, and Rita became an Augustinian nun in 1413. She had persevered, prayed, and—through the intercession of St. John the Baptist, St. Augustine, and St. Nicholas of Tolentino—eventually received what she desired.

† Rita's life is an incredible example of perseverance. She didn't give up on her husband, her sons, or becoming a nun. May we persevere in God's will like Rita, even when the way forward seems impossible.

DAY 5

In the convent, Rita practiced the same humble patience that had helped convert her husband and sons. She especially cared for her fellow nuns who were sick, and for the Christians who, like her husband, did not take seriously their relationship with Jesus or their practice of the faith. Many souls were converted through her prayer, persuasion, and penance.

† What zeal Rita had for souls! She always worked for others to know the deep love of Jesus Christ. Who in your life should you be especially praying and suffering for right now? Ask Jesus to show you how you might best encourage them to live a holy life.

DAY 6

From her childhood, Rita had a devotion to the passion (that is, the sufferings) of Jesus. In 1441, she received a special gift of a share in His passion. As she knelt in prayer after a sermon on the crown of thorns, she felt intense pain in her forehead, as if a thorn had detached itself from the crucifix and pierced her there. From then on, this physical and mystical wound remained with Rita. It festered so much that she had to be secluded from the other sisters, but as the sisters prepared to take a pilgrimage to Rome, Rita begged that Jesus would heal her long enough to make the trip. The wound was healed for the length of their pilgrimage and returned when they arrived home, remaining until her death in 1457.

† Thank God for your sufferings today, because each suffering is a kiss from Jesus on the cross, uniting us more closely to Him in His passion.

DAY 7

At the time of her death, Rita asked for a rose from her old garden. Although it wasn't the season for roses, her friend went to the garden and found a rosebush in full bloom. He picked a flower, brought it to her, and asked if he could do anything else. She asked for two figs from the garden. Again, he went out to the garden and found a fig tree with no leaves but two ripe figs.

† Jesus always gives us what we need. He does not always give us what we want, but He is conscious of all our needs. Even in the midst of His kisses from the cross, Jesus provides us with the sweet little things that help keep us focused and motivated. Think of the little things in life that bring you joy today and thank God for them.

St. Bede the Venerable

Priest and Doctor of the Church

Patron saint of historians and those who write in English

FEAST DAY: May 25

DAY 1

Bede (pronounced "beed"), who lived from AD 673 to 735, was a priest, monk, and scholar, perhaps the most learned man in the world during his time. Not only is he one of the best theologians in history, having been declared a Doctor of the Church by Pope Leo XIII, he is also known as the "father of English history," having written the first comprehensive history of the English: *The Ecclesiastical History of the English People.* He was also instrumental in calculating the number of years since the birth of Christ and in explaining the calculation of the date of Easter each year. These calculations still influence everyone's lives today, Christian and non-Christian alike.

† It is amazing how the work of one person can affect the lives of others—for good or for ill—even more than 1,000 years later. What kind of legacy do you want to leave? Most of us won't affect the whole world, but all of us can affect some of those who come after us.

DAY 2

In 673, Bede was born in a small village in the kingdom of Northumbria (the very northern portion of modern-day England). The very next year, St. Benedict Biscop founded the Benedictine abbey of St. Peter's at Wearmouth, less than 10 miles away. In 680, he founded the abbey of St. Paul's so close to Bede's home that the village came to be considered part of abbey property.

† The Bible tells us that "in everything God works for good with those who love him, who are called according to his purpose" (Romans 8:28). The seemingly random circumstance of Bede's birth at nearly the same time as the founding of these monasteries offered him a trajectory for his entire life. Which seemingly random circumstances of your life have afforded you the choices to get you where you are today?

DAY 3

Bede was entrusted to the care of St. Benedict Biscop at the age of seven and, from that time on, was blessed with the best of teachers. In addition to Benedict, Bede also learned from the monk Trumbert, the abbot Adrian, and Theodorus, the archbishop of Canterbury. He learned church music—chant—from the man who had previously been in charge of music for the pope himself at St. Peter's in Rome. Bede was ordained a deacon at only 19. Then, after continuing in his studies for 11 more years, he was ordained a priest in 702 by St. John of Beverley.

† Who has taught you, formally or informally? Thank God for them today, then think of a way to pass on their legacy by teaching others.

DAY 4

The motto of the Benedictine monks is *Ora et Labora,* Latin for "prayer and work." While the spiritual work of prayer, sacrifice, and love is most important (which is why prayer comes before work in the motto), St. Benedict saw clearly the value of manual labor for his monks. For all healthy monks, there is at least some manual labor. Bede therefore also performed tasks like shucking corn, milking livestock, and baking bread.

† Bede was humble enough to do manual work for the good of his brother monks and himself. What physical work do you do that blesses your family? Think of simple things like mopping the floor or washing the dishes. Let this work be an act of love for your family.

DAY 5

Bede's main focus, however, was not on scholarship but on Jesus Christ. All of his writing and all of his work was meant to give glory to God. He was able to focus deeply no matter what he was doing, knowing that he was doing it both with and for Jesus. As *Lives of the Saints* author Father Alban Butler wrote, "To see him pray, says an ancient writer, one would have thought he left himself no time to study; and when we look at his books we admire he could have found time to do anything else but write."

† With so many technological distractions today, it seems harder than ever to stay focused. Take five slow, deep breaths as you put this book down. Try to do so multiple times throughout the day.

DAY 6

Not only did Bede write but, in the footsteps of the great teachers who had taught him, he also ran a school for fellow monks and for others. One of his students, Ecgbert, became bishop of York and went on to teach Alcuin. Alcuin then became the leading educational adviser to Charlemagne and thus one of the most significant influences on the educational program of the Middle Ages.

✝ Simply reading this book shows that you are part of a privileged segment of the human family: You can read! Most people in the history of the world haven't been able to. You have vast libraries of human knowledge at your fingertips on the internet. Thank God for these gifts and be sure to use them well.

DAY 7

In April of 735, Bede—now 61 or 62 years old—began to have trouble breathing. Giving thanks to God for his life, he continued to pray and study. Every day, he taught his students and sang the Psalms with his hands extended in prayer. As he suffered and prayed and taught during these last 50 days or so of his life, Bede translated into English St. Isidore's *Etymologiae* (which we learned about a few weeks ago) and the Gospel according to John.

✝ Bede's life ended much like it had always been: in peace, prayer, tranquility, and work. There are no miracles to speak of during his life, nor any extravagant signs. He simply prayed and worked, faithfully using his gifts from God. May we do the same!

St. Charles Lwanga & Companions

Martyrs

Patron saints of African Catholic Youth Action, converts, and torture victims

FEAST DAY: June 3

DAY 1

In 1879, the Society of the Missionaries of Africa arrived in the kingdom of Buganda (in what is now Uganda) and were peacefully received by King Mutesa. Soon, many people began to become Catholic, including many young men in the king's court.

† Beginning with the Apostles themselves, Christians have always generously and courageously followed Jesus's final command to "make disciples of all nations" (Matthew 28:19). How are you following Jesus's command to make disciples?

DAY 2

When King Mutesa died, however, his son Mwanga took the throne. Mwanga's wicked deeds included sexually abusing young men in his court. The chief page, a Catholic named Joseph Mukasa, worked very hard to protect the young boys. After he spoke out against Mwanga's murder of a visiting Anglican bishop, he was beheaded for his faith on November 15, 1885.

† So many wicked and horrible things happen in this world: the abuse of children, vulnerable adults, and spouses; human trafficking; murder; racism. Take five minutes in silent prayer today. As you begin, beg Jesus to heal this wickedness. Then, simply ask him if you're supposed to do something about it—fasting, financial support, advocacy, or the like.

DAY 3

On the night of Mukasa's murder, the young men and boys in the king's court went to the Missionaries of Africa (also known as the "White Fathers" because of the color of their habits) and asked to be baptized. With their lives also endangered by the murderous lust of the king, they were baptized that very night. Following the words of Jesus Himself, these young men knew the meaning of the gift of baptism: "Unless one is born of water and the Spirit, he cannot enter the Kingdom of God" (John 3:5).

† Thank God for the gift of your baptism today. If you can, take a little pilgrimage to the church where you were baptized to thank Him.

DAY 4

With Joseph's death, Charles Lwanga, a newly baptized man of 25, succeeded Joseph in his role as chief page. He, too, was a Catholic who dedicated himself to accompanying the young disciples in their walk with Jesus and vigorously protecting them from the king. Months later, King Mwanga was furious when one of the boys resisted his advances because the boy was learning his catechism. The king questioned all the young men in the court, and 15 of them stepped forward as Christians. When he asked if they were willing to keep the faith, they replied, "Until death!"

† These young men knew the same truth as another young saint, Joan of Arc, who said shortly before her death, "I would rather die than do a thing which I know to be a sin or against the will of God." Ask these Ugandan martyrs to pray for you today that you might have the courage to avoid sin, especially mortal sin.

DAY 5

The young men were tied to each other and made to march for two days to the place where they were to be burned at the stake. On the march, one of these martyrs shouted out, "God will rescue me. But you will not see how he does it, because he will take my soul and leave you only my body." The guards cut him to pieces on the spot and left him dying on the road by himself.

† This martyr's words speak of a great confidence in God. Yes, we will receive our bodies again. But our bodies are not yet immortal until the Second Coming. Our souls are immortal. Perform a checkup on the state of your soul. Examine your conscience and go to confession.

DAY 6

Upon reaching the site of their martyrdom, the young men were made to suffer more by remaining tied together for seven days while the guards prepared the wood for the fire. On June 3, 1886 (the Feast of the Ascension), Charles Lwanga was separated from the rest and burned at the stake alone. From the midst of the flames, just before death, he cried out to God in the Luganda language. "*Katonda!*" he proclaimed, which means "My God!" or, more literally, "Creator!" Then he passed into the hands of our Father. Most of the other martyrs were burned together on that same day, praying and singing as they died. In all, there were 22 Ugandan "protomartyrs"—the first martyrs in a particular region.

† The trust of these martyrs is incredible. How did they do it? They were empowered by the Holy Spirit. Pray to the Holy Spirit today, asking for trust and courage like these martyrs had.

DAY 7

Today, 500,000 people gather each year in Namugongo, Uganda, at the spot where these first martyrs were executed. According to the Center for the Study of Global Christianity, there are more than 600 million Christians in Africa, and Uganda is one of the world's most Catholic countries. The early Christian Tertullian, watching the persecution of the first Christians at the hands of the Romans, wrote these words, a fitting commentary on how the Church triumphs over the world not with swords and spears but with prayer and sacrifice: "We are not a new philosophy but a divine revelation. That's why you can't just exterminate us; the more you kill the more we are. The blood of the martyrs is the seed of the church . . . and you frustrate your purpose. Because those who see us die, wonder why we do . . . and when they find out, they join us."

† Remember today that God always wins. Even when His Church seems defeated, she always comes through by the grace of His resurrection.

St. Anthony of Padua

Priest and Doctor of the Church

Patron saint of Lisbon, Portugal; lost items, people, and souls; amputees; and devotion to Jesus in the Blessed Sacrament; among others

FEAST DAY: June 13

DAY 1

Despite the name by which he's come to be known, St. Anthony of Padua was born Fernando Martins de Bulhões in Lisbon, Portugal, in 1195. His parents sent him to school at the local cathedral in Lisbon, where he proved to be both a gifted student and a devout disciple of Christ. At just 15 years old, he entered the religious community there, becoming a brother in the Augustinian Order. As a brother, he continued to work hard at his studies, reading the Bible and the church fathers constantly. Through his hard work and natural gifts, he became a great speaker, but he continued in a humble life of prayer and study for a decade.

† We tend to think that talents like Anthony's knowledge or eloquence come without effort. The truth is that the best in the world both have natural talent and invest in their talents with hard work. Read Matthew 25:14–30 today and make a plan for working hard, like Anthony, to invest in the talents God has given you.

DAY 2

When Fernando was about 25 years old, a priest brought to his city the relics of five friars of the new Franciscan Order who had been martyred while preaching in Morocco. The Franciscans set up a small house near where Fernando lived, asking for the patronage of St. Anthony of the Desert (whom we met in week 4). Inspired by the example of these new martyrs, Fernando found himself with a strong and growing desire to lay down his own life for Christ.

† Jesus died for you and me. Therefore, the best way for us to be close to Jesus is to be willing to die for Him. "No one has greater love than this," Jesus said, "than to lay down one's life for one's friends" (John 15:13).

DAY 3

With Franciscan friars now living nearby, Fernando also felt a growing desire to live the kind of simple, radical life the Franciscans were living. Begging the Holy Spirit for guidance, Fernando heard and followed a call from God to leave the Augustinian Order and join the Franciscan Order. Receiving permission from his superiors, he joined the Franciscans in 1221 and took the name Anthony, asking St. Anthony of the Desert to be one of his patron saints.

† Remember your patron saints? If you're named after a saint, that saint is happy to pray for you. But don't forget that, like Anthony, you can ask any saint to be a patron for you. And you can have more than one! Ask your patron saints for intercession today. Or ask a new saint to take you under his or her patronage.

DAY 4

After some time in solitude, prayer, and penance, Anthony asked permission to depart for Africa, where he was convinced he would find martyrdom. It was not Anthony's vocation, however, to be a martyr. Soon after his arrival in Morocco, he became seriously ill and had to return to Spain to recover. His ship to Spain, however, was driven off course by bad weather and landed in Sicily, where Anthony learned that St. Francis was holding a large meeting of Franciscans in Assisi. Sick as he was, he made his way to Assisi, where he met St. Francis and offered to remain in Italy serving as a friar.

† Oftentimes it seems that our lives are driven off course. But how much less anxious and worried would we be if we trusted God to use these detours for our good like He did for Anthony? Turn to page 210 and pray the Litany of Trust today.

DAY 5

Since no one in Italy knew of Anthony's great knowledge and preaching talent, he was able to devote himself all the more to prayer, penance, and solitude while serving in the kitchen. But when a group of Dominican and Franciscan friars gathered together and it came time for the homily, a mix-up occurred: The Franciscans thought that one of the Dominicans would be preaching, and vice versa. Since no one else was prepared to do it, Anthony's superior ordered him to preach, proclaiming to everyone whatever the Holy Spirit would put into his mouth. Anthony was outed as a superb public speaker!

† Anthony's life of prayer, study, and quiet service had prepared him for this moment. All he had left to do was to trust. When opportunities arise for us to speak God's Word in the simple situations of our daily lives, may we trust courageously like Anthony!

DAY 6

With his talents on display for all to see, Anthony was soon asked to pursue further studies in theology at the university, then teach his brother Franciscans, eventually ending up as a provincial superior. St. Francis wrote Anthony the shortest and wisest of letters: "I am pleased that you teach sacred theology to the brothers providing that, as is contained in the Rule, you 'do not extinguish the Spirit of prayer and devotion' during study of this kind." While study is good, it can never replace prayer. The goal of life, the saints know, is not to do or know great things but to live in communion with the divine, personal God who has revealed Himself to the world in the incarnation of our Lord Jesus Christ.

† It is very easy to put things that feel urgent before those that are most important. We have to be careful not to put our work *for* God ahead of our relationship *with* God. Devote five extra minutes to prayer today. Use Luke 10:41–42, if you'd like.

DAY 7

Now employed with preaching and teaching, Anthony devoted himself to this new mission entrusted to him by God. For teaching, he had, among other things, a book of the Psalms (known as a Psalter) with his lecture notes in it. Unfortunately, a novice friar suddenly left the community and took Anthony's Psalter with him. Anthony prayed that it would be returned, and, aided by the grace of his intercession, the thief both returned the book and rejoined the order. This is why Anthony is the patron saint of those who have lost things.

† God cared about Anthony's book, but he cared more about the good of the person responsible for the lost book. Offer some mortification—some sacrifice such as skipping coffee or avoiding snacks between meals—for a person who is spiritually lost.

St. Aloysius Gonzaga

Religious brother

Patron saint of young students, Christian youth, Jesuit scholastics, those who are blind, AIDS patients, and caregivers to AIDS patients

FEAST DAY: June 21

DAY 1

Aloysius was the son of two Italians noble in their birth and in their piety. When Aloysius's father asked his mother to marry him, she took time for fasting and prayer to learn the will of God and, after resolving to say yes to her future husband, to ask God's blessing upon their marriage. After their marriage, she begged God for a son who would devote himself entirely to His service. God granted her request, and she gave birth to Aloysius on March 9, 1568.

† When she wanted to know the will of God, Aloysius's mother fasted and prayed. She didn't simply wish that God would show her something. Instead, she opened the ears of her heart by this fasting and prayer. When we are in discernment (prayerful consideration), may we do the same!

DAY 2

In answer to his mother's prayers, Aloysius was filled with deep piety and love for the poor from a very young age. As early as possible, she taught him the names of Jesus and Mary, the sign of the cross, and the parts of the catechism he could understand. He responded to this teaching and was often found immersed in simple but deep prayer in some private place in the house. Around the age of seven, he began to pray from the book of Psalms on his knees without a cushion.

† In Aloysius we see extraordinarily displayed a reality that is true for each of us. We are each called by God to be saints from the first moment of our creation. Today, follow Aloysius's example of praying with the Psalms, and reflect on Psalm 139.

DAY 3

Encouraged by reading a little book on the rosary, Aloysius's devotion to the Blessed Mother was deepened, and he seems to have asked for and received a gift of perfect chastity such that he was never in his life tempted to lust. This gift, however, did not stop Aloysius from working for chastity and the other virtues. He continued in prayer, in mortification, and in fleeing immediately from the near occasion of sin. He was humble enough to know the weakness of his own fallen human nature, which could be knocked off course by the slightest breeze of temptation.

† What is your favorite sin? What are you going to do about it? Make a plan this week. First, ask the Holy Spirit to guide you. Then, plan out how you will pray against the sin; perform mortifications that act against it; and avoid times, places, or people that make it easier to fall into that sin.

DAY 4

When he was only 11, Aloysius decided to cede his rights as firstborn son to his younger brother Rodolfo so that he could be more completely devoted to Jesus. Not long after, Aloysius fell seriously ill for the second time in his life. His first sickness had lasted 18 months, and this one wasn't short either. He could have complained or felt sorry for himself. But this 12-year-old boy instead chose to spend more time alone with Jesus, reading holy books and praying.

† God uses every event in our lives—even the bad ones—as an opportunity for our good. Open your Bible, read Romans 8:28, and think about how you, like Aloysius, might open your soul to the good God promises to do, even in difficult times.

DAY 5

Another book soon made a profound impact on Aloysius. This time it was a book on the lives of priests and brothers serving as missionaries in the West Indies. Reading their writings and learning of their lives, Aloysius was inspired with a desire to join the Society of Jesus (the religious order commonly known as the Jesuits) with the mission of saving souls.

† Books can change our lives. A change in one's life begins with a change in one's thoughts, and good books can spark new, good thoughts. Think of something you want to know more about or a struggle you're having, and find a book on the topic.

DAY 6

In 1580, 12-year-old Aloysius was blessed to meet St. Charles Borromeo, Cardinal Archbishop of Milan, who was impressed by the boy's piety and devotion. Learning that Aloysius had not yet received First Communion, Charles encouraged him to prepare himself, receive Communion for the first time, and to do so frequently from then on. Inspired by the great saint, Aloysius fostered a deep and tender devotion to Jesus in the Blessed Sacrament, which, according to Father Alban Butler, became "his greatest comfort and joy."

✝ Is the Blessed Sacrament a comfort and joy for you? Jesus is there waiting for you in the tabernacle! Following Aloysius, make a visit to your local church this week to spend time with Jesus in the Blessed Sacrament, especially if there is adoration.

DAY 7

At 13, Aloysius made his final resolution to enter the Society of Jesus, which was confirmed by his priest confessor, who guided him in spiritual matters. Although his father was initially opposed, he eventually gave Aloysius his blessing, and Aloysius was sent to Rome. Around five years later, an epidemic broke out in Rome. The Jesuits erected a hospital in which the highest-ranking priests served the sick. Aloysius begged to join them and, after being allowed in, focused earnestly on caring for the poor. He cared for their bodies—and for their souls, by teaching them the Christian faith. On March 3, 1591, Aloysius caught the disease and took to his bed. That June, he went to meet the Lord, the last word to pass from his lips being the holy name of Jesus.

✝ To pray the name of Jesus is to ask God to save us. That is, after all, what the name Jesus means—"God saves"! Repeat the name of Jesus as you go about your day today. Make it a quiet and reverent prayer.

St. Peter & St. Paul

Apostles

Patron saints of fishermen and preachers, among many other things

FEAST DAY: June 29

DAY 1

With St. Peter and St. Paul, we come to another double feast day! These might just be the two most important men among the early Christians (followed closely by James and John). Peter was the Prince of the Apostles. Paul, the greatest missionary in the history of the world, probably didn't even meet Jesus until after the resurrection.

† The "yeses" of these two men changed history. They didn't just say yes to the Lord one time and stop there. The giant yes of their entire lives was made up of countless small yeses and punctuated by a few particularly big ones. How can you say yes to Jesus in your life today?

DAY 2

We first meet Peter, whose given name was Simon, with his brother Andrew. Andrew was a disciple of John the Baptist, who pointed him to Jesus. Andrew had the courage to follow Jesus and to invite his brother Simon to join him. "We have found the Messiah!" Andrew exclaimed (John 1:41–42). And Simon, following him, encountered the Lord and received his new name: Peter.

† Peter trusted Andrew enough to listen to him. Before encountering Jesus, he had to connect with another person who brought him to Jesus. How can you be like Andrew? Whom in your life can you bring to Jesus? That person, very normal and flawed, might become a great saint like Peter.

DAY 3

Peter journeyed with Jesus for three years, was made the steward of the Kingdom of God (Matthew 16:18–19), denied Jesus at His hour of greatest need (Luke 22:54–62), and was later restored to grace, being affirmed in his identity as shepherd after the heart of Christ (John 21). After the resurrection and ascension of our Lord, it was Peter who preached the first Christian sermon, inviting the crowd to "repent, and be baptized every one of you in the name of Jesus Christ for the forgiveness of your sins" (Acts 2:38). Three thousand souls were saved that day, responding to Peter's Spirit-filled preaching.

† People often ask why we don't see occurrences like those in Acts of the Apostles today. I think it's because we don't ask for the Holy Spirit. Sure, we pray, but as James tells us in the Bible, "You do not have, because you do not ask. You ask and do not receive, because you ask wrongly, to spend it on your passions" (James 4:2-3). Let us ask for the Holy Spirit to come upon us, that we might know, love, and do His will with joy.

DAY 4

We first meet Saul (who would more often be called Paul) at the murder of the very first Christian martyr: Stephen the Deacon. The Bible makes it clear that Saul was present and, although he seems not to have directly killed Stephen, he "was consenting to his death" (Acts 8:1). While devout men buried Stephen, Saul did the opposite. He "laid waste the Church, and entering house after house, he dragged off men and women and committed them to prison" (Acts 8:3). Saul had good intentions but was, in truth, doing what his teacher Gamaliel had warned against. Gamaliel had reminded the council of the men prior to Jesus who had claimed to be the Messiah. Each of them had been put to death, and in each case, their followers had dispersed. "So," Gamaliel said, "in the present case I tell you, keep away from these men and let them alone; for if this plan or this undertaking is of men, it will fail; but if it is from God, you will not be able to overthrow them. You might even be found opposing God!" (Acts 5:38–39).

† Of all the men claiming to be the Messiah, Jesus is the only one who rose from the dead and the only one who still has followers. May we follow Him faithfully, even when we are persecuted.

DAY 5

Saul found Himself, in Gamaliel's words, "opposing God" (Acts 5:39), and God was about to make that very clear to him. While he was on the road to the city of Damascus to continue laying waste to the Church, Jesus Christ appeared to him. "Saul, Saul, why are you persecuting me?" said the Lord. "I am Jesus, whom you are persecuting" (Acts 9:4–5). Struck temporarily blind by Jesus, Saul was led by the hand into Damascus, where he fasted and prayed.

† When Saul was suffering, he entered into prayer and fasting, even though suffering usually makes us want to "check out." The next time you suffer, try to increase your prayer and sacrifice like Paul.

DAY 6

As Saul prayed and fasted, God spoke to a disciple in Damascus named Ananias, who, though afraid, obeyed God, laying hands on Saul to restore his sight and baptizing him. "Brother Saul," he said, "the Lord Jesus who appeared to you on the road by which you came, has sent me that you may regain your sight and be filled with the Holy Spirit" (Acts 9:17). Saul's sight was restored, and by baptism he was filled with the Holy Spirit. He began to witness to Jesus Christ, the Son of God, in Damascus.

† Stephen had, like Jesus, prayed for God to forgive his murderers. God heard his prayer and extended forgiveness to Saul. But the rest of the Church still had to live the hard task of forgiveness. Put yourself in Ananias's place. Could you have forgiven Saul? Ask for the grace to forgive your enemies today. That is necessary for a Christian.

DAY 7

After escaping from an assassination attempt in Damascus, Saul took three years away from everyday life in retreat—perhaps journeying even to Mount Sinai, where Moses had received the Ten Commandments from God (see Galatians 4:25)—and was brought back into the apostolic ministry when "Barnabas went to Tarsus to look for Saul" (Acts 11:25). Often referring to himself as Paul (his Greek name), he began—first with Barnabas, then with others—to preach the salvation of our Lord Jesus Christ all around the ancient Mediterranean world, even in the capital of Rome and perhaps as far as Spain, the edge of the continent. Paul, the great persecutor of the Church, had become the great evangelizer of the world!

† Paul's mission flowed from his relationship with God. He took time away from the mission to seek the "one thing necessary" (Luke 10:42). When is the last time you went on retreat? Look at your calendar this week and do your best to schedule time for a weekend retreat within the next six months. Ask your parish priest if you need help finding one.

WEEK 27

St. Thomas

Apostle

Patron saint of India

FEAST DAY: July 3

DAY 1

Sometimes called "doubting Thomas," this Apostle was a man of great courage and, eventually, of great faith. We first hear Thomas speak in John 11:16. Lazarus was dead, and in order to reach him, Jesus had to journey through territory controlled by people who wanted to kill him. The Apostles were confused and perhaps a little scared. But Thomas, the Bible tells us, said to his fellow disciples, "Let us also go, that we may die with him." Thomas didn't know what he was getting into, but he had such devotion to Jesus that he would follow Him even to death.

† Are you willing to die with Him? Are you willing to have an uncomfortable conversation or to stand up for what's right, even when it's hard? Ask Thomas to pray for you today that you might have this kind of zeal.

DAY 2

The disciples were not called to die with Jesus—at least not yet—and we hear from Thomas again in John 14:5. As Jesus continued to reveal to His disciples the mysteries of His desire to bring them to the Father's house, Thomas responded with deep innocence and deep honesty: "Lord, we do not know where you are going; how can we know the way?" To that, Jesus replied, "I am the way, and the truth, and the life; no one comes to the Father, but by me" (14:6). From this, we see that Jesus is the only way into the Kingdom of Heaven.

† How deeply do you desire, like Thomas, to be where Jesus is? And how deeply do you desire for other people also to be where Jesus is? Pray today for those who do not know Jesus, and perhaps offer a fast or some other little sacrifice for them.

DAY 3

We next meet Thomas in the incident for which he is most famous. On Easter Sunday, Jesus appeared to the disciples, but Thomas was not with them. When they told him the miraculous, joyous news of Jesus's resurrection, Thomas responded with incredulity: "Unless I see in his hands the print of the nails, and place my finger in the mark of the nails, and place my hand in his side, I will not believe" (John 20:25).

† Thomas was 100 percent honest—with his friends, with his emotions, and probably in his prayer to God. Sometimes we believe the lie that we have to have it all together to be Christians. But nothing could be further from the truth! Could you be more honest about your thoughts, feelings, and desires in your prayer to God?

DAY 4

The next week, Jesus came to His disciples again, and Thomas was with them this time. Quoting Thomas from the week before, Jesus said to him, "Put your finger here, and see my hands; and put out your hand, and place it in my side; do not be faithless, but believing" (John 20:27). Then follows the climax of the entire Gospel according to John, in which Thomas declares the truth of Jesus's identity: "My Lord and my God!" (John 20:28). As Pope St. Gregory the Great preached so many years ago, "the incredulity of Thomas was more useful for our faith than the faith of the disciples who believed."

† It is a venerable custom to repeat the words of Thomas when the priest holds up the body and blood of Christ at Mass. Try it the next time you go to Mass. As the priest elevates the sacred host and the sacred chalice, say under your breath, "My Lord and my God!"

DAY 5

Soon after the ascension of Christ, according to the historian Eusebius, Thomas sent one of the 70 (Luke 10:1–12) named Thaddaeus to Agbar, the powerful king of the important city of Edessa, who suffered from a disease. "I have believed," Agbar confessed, "both in [Jesus] and in his Father." At that, Thaddaeus replied, "I place my hand upon thee in the name of the same Lord Jesus," and the king was immediately healed.

† No physical healing comes without a spiritual healing. First, Agbar was given the gift of faith. Then he was given the gift of a healing. God is first concerned with the deeper, spiritual things that determine whether we live with Him forever in heaven or whether we choose to turn away from Him and imprison ourselves in hell. May we, like King Agbar, receive deeply the gift of faith, and then, if it is what's best for us, may we receive any physical healing for which we ask.

DAY 6

Thomas's zeal to preach the gospel took him far and wide. Today it's difficult to separate fact from fiction in the post-biblical mission of Thomas, but he most likely made his way through ancient Persia all the way to the coast of India. St. Ephrem and others indicate that he was martyred there, many say at the point of a spear or a lance. A basilica is built there upon the site of his original tomb, where, in 1523, an archeological excavation found a chapel with what seemed to be at least some of Thomas's bones, along with a piece of the lance with which he was martyred and a vial containing some of his blood.

† Remember today the power of the intercession of the saints through their relics. Read Acts 19:11–12 and 2 Kings 13:21 today, giving glory to God for the miracles He works through the clothes and the bones of the saints.

DAY 7

The hymns of St. Ephrem the Syrian indicate that Thomas was martyred in India and that, later, some of his relics were carried to Edessa, where, as we learned on day 5, he had sent Thaddaeus many years before to cure King Agbar. St. Ephrem wrote, "The Evil One wailed 'Where now, is there a place for me to flee to from the righteous? I stirred up Death to slay the Apostles, that I might be safe from their blows. By their deaths now more exceedingly am I cruelly beaten. The Apostle whom I slew in India is before me in Edessa: he is here wholly and also there. I went there, there was he: here and there I have found him and been grieved.'"

† The faithful sacrifices of the saints are united to the cross of Christ and, being united to the cross, stop the devil in his tracks. That goes for your sacrifices, too. Love Jesus. Be courageous. Stop the devil in his tracks!

WEEK 28

St. Maria Goretti

Virgin and martyr

Patron saint of teenage girls, modern youth, victims of rape, and victims of crime

FEAST DAY: July 6

DAY 1

When Maria Goretti was young, her father, a farmer, died of malaria, and her mother worked hard to support their six children. As the eldest daughter, Maria took care of the household while her mother and most of her siblings worked the fields. Although she was living in deep poverty, Maria prayed the rosary nightly that her father might be in heaven with Jesus, and she lived with a cheerfulness noticed by all. "God will provide," she would gently remind her mother.

† Maria had deep trust and engaged in deep prayer. She neither presumed that her father was in heaven nor despaired of his salvation. Following Maria's example, offer a rosary today for someone who has passed away. Pray this rosary in a cemetery if possible.

DAY 2

When Maria was around 10 years old, she began to beg her mother to allow her to make her First Communion. But her mother, busy with work and worried about the cost of a proper First Communion dress, kept putting it off. Eventually, Maria received permission from her mother to seek out someone to teach her the catechism, and within 11 months, she was prepared to receive Jesus for the first time. "God will provide," she again said to her mother, and God did—for her catechism and even for the external trappings, including a dress, earrings, a necklace, a candle, shoes, and a borrowed veil.

† Maria had great faith in God. Think of some area in your life where you need Him to provide. Then, like Maria, both pray for His help and work toward that goal.

DAY 3

After Maria received her first Holy Communion, her mother told her, "Now you will be very good, because you have received Jesus." And she responded, "Yes, Mom, I'll always be very good!" Maria kept her promise, striving to be a comforting angel to her mother and caring for the family's cooking, cleaning, and sewing needs.

† Our reception of Holy Communion, since it is a reception of God Himself, is meant to be a source of healing and strength for us. Jesus comes Himself, under the appearances of bread and wine, to be our manna from heaven, strengthening us on our journey to the Promised Land. The next time you receive Holy Communion at Mass, think of a situation in which you often fail to do good, and beg Jesus for healing there.

DAY 4

Due to their poverty, the Goretti family had to share a house with the Serenelli family, including the 20-year-old Alessandro. Alessandro had corrupted his mind with indecent—possibly even pornographic—reading and bad examples. As he put it prior to his death, "a violent force blinded me and pushed me toward a wrong way of life." In June of 1902, he made sexual advances toward the 12-year-old Maria, which she flatly rejected. Alessandro threatened to kill her. After a second wicked advance, which she also rejected, he determined to murder her if she again rejected him, preparing a 10-inch awl for the job.

† What is the greatest source of lust in your life? Ask Maria for her intercession, and consider sharing your struggle with someone you trust. If you struggle with pornography, visit Matt Fradd's free website, Strive21, and begin your journey to freedom.

DAY 5

After a month of verbal and emotional abuse, Alessandro contrived to get Maria alone. As Alessandro told it before his death: "I brutally grabbed her by the arm and, as she was resisting, dragged her into the kitchen . . . [S]he told me: No, no, God does not want this. If you do this you go to hell. Seeing that she was determined to reject my brutal cravings, I went on a rampage, took the bradawl and began to stab her in the stomach . . . As I was stabbing her, she struggled to defend herself and repeatedly invoked the name of her mother and cried out: God, God, I'm dying, Mom, Mom! . . . I understood that I had mortally wounded her. I threw the weapon behind the caisson and I went into my bedroom. I locked the door and threw myself on the bed."

† What a wicked, sad, and horrible story, yet one that is all too common. Pray for those who suffer or have suffered from rape, abuse, or domestic violence. Maybe there is a shelter in your area that you could assist in some way.

DAY 6

Found by her family, Maria was rushed to the hospital, where she survived for 24 hours. In the midst of much suffering and prayer, she received the last rites, including Holy Communion, which had brought her such great joy. Reminded of the words of Jesus forgiving His own executioners, Maria exclaimed of Alessandro, "Yes, for the love of Jesus, I forgive him and I want him to be in paradise with me."

† What Christlike forgiveness Maria extended to her murderer! Can we do the same? Pray the Our Father slowly today, truly asking God to "forgive those who trespass against us."

DAY 7

Upon her death, Maria was immediately acclaimed as a martyr and a saint. Only two years after her martyrdom, a marble monument was dedicated to her, and her first biography was published. Alessandro, for his part, showed no remorse for his sin until eight years into his prison sentence, when, one night, Maria appeared to him in a dream. Dressed in white, she offered 14 white lilies to him, one for each stab wound he had inflicted on her. When he awoke, Alessandro repented and changed his life. When he was eventually released from prison, he immediately went to Maria's mother to beg for her forgiveness, which she gave him. How could she not, she said, when Maria herself had forgiven him from her deathbed? Alessandro lived the rest of his days as a laborer at a Franciscan monastery and eventually as a lay brother.

† No matter what you have done—even murder—you can find forgiveness and healing. Ask for forgiveness, approach the sacrament of confession, and know that you, too, can become a saint!

St. Kateri Tekakwitha

Virgin

Patron saint of Indigenous Americans; the environment; and people who lose their parents, are in exile, or are ridiculed for their piety

FEAST DAY: July 14

DAY 1

In what is now known as Auriesville, New York, Tekakwitha was born—like St. Augustine and multiple other saints—to a Christian mother and a non-Christian father. Her mother was a member of the Algonquin tribe, and her father a member of the Mohawk tribe. Unfortunately, both of them, along with their infant son, were among the 44,000 Indigenous Americans who died in the 1660 smallpox epidemic. Although four-year-old Tekakwitha survived the disease, her face was scarred and her sight was significantly affected (her name means "she who bumps into things"). She resolved to be completely devoted to Jesus for her whole life, and she resisted when, at eight years old, she was paired to be married. Her mother must have taught her about Jesus when she was a very little girl—truths she never forgot, even though she had not yet received the gift of baptism.

† Thank God today for the person who first showed you the love of Jesus.

DAY 2

Tekakwitha lived with her uncle after her parents' deaths. When she was 11 years old, three Jesuit missionaries came to the village, and although Tekakwitha's uncle didn't want her to have any contact with them, they made a deep impact on her. When their village was attacked by Mohican warriors a couple years later, Tekakwitha and other girls helped one of the priests take care of the wounded, bury the dead, and feed the warriors. When the villagers won the battle and began to torture captured enemy combatants, the Jesuits pleaded for mercy upon them.

✝ Compassion, common service, and love for enemies are hallmarks of Christians. While she was helping and watching the Jesuits, Tekakwitha had made no formal study of the catechism. She was learning from the living catechism of the Christians in her life. Be a living catechism for others to see!

DAY 3

At 18, Tekakwitha continued to resist societal pressures to marry and secretly began official lessons in the Christian faith. Eventually, her family gave up their resistance and consented to her becoming a Christian by baptism on Easter Sunday 1676. At baptism, she took the name Kateri, after St. Catherine of Siena. Our saint had taken a patron saint!

✝ Taking a patron saint is one of the oldest and most common practices among Christians. Maybe Tekakwitha identified with Catherine of Siena's family's resistance to her being a consecrated virgin. Have you identified with a particular saint in journeying through this book? Don't forget to ask them to pray for you (in addition to the saint chosen for you at your baptism and the saint you may have chosen at your confirmation). Maybe get a prayer card with that saint and use it as your bookmark for this book, praying the prayer on the back each day when you do your reading.

DAY 4

Her baptism and her family's consent did not, however, spare Kateri from the harassment of many in her community. She was even falsely accused of wrongdoing and threatened with death. As a result, she fled to the Mission of St. Francis Xavier, 200 miles away, and received the title "Lily of the Mohawks" from the people there who saw her great faith, kindness, and resilience. On Christmas Day 1677, she received Holy Communion for the first time.

† Some saints are called to remain in this kind of persecution and become holy through it. Other saints, like Kateri, are able to escape to a better life. They become holy through that, praise God! Today, read Psalm 23 and thank God for the times He has led you to better pastures through suffering.

DAY 5

Although she was devoted to Jesus, there was still much Kateri didn't know. At the mission, however, she met Anastasia Tegonhatsiongo, who had been a friend of her mother's. She also became close friends with Maria Thérèse Tegaianguenta and many other women who supported each other in their journey as disciples of Jesus. This community of women nourished Kateri's spiritual life and helped her draw even closer to Jesus.

† The book of Acts gives us the formula for Christian life: "They devoted themselves to the teaching of the apostles and to the communal life, to the breaking of the bread and to the prayers" (2:42). Be vulnerable and share your faith with someone else or a group of friends who might be willing to support each other in living as disciples of Jesus Christ. Pray instead of gossiping. Build others up instead of tearing them down.

DAY 6

On the Feast of the Ascension in 1679, Kateri's long-held desire to be completely given over to Jesus was sealed by a vow of perpetual virginity. "I have deliberated enough," she said. "For a long time my decision on what I will do has been made. I have consecrated myself entirely to Jesus, son of Mary, I have chosen Him for husband and He alone will take me for wife." Kateri, like a great host of holy women before and after her, had become a consecrated virgin, the first among Indigenous Americans. Having been given this special grace by God, she followed the words of Jesus himself in choosing the Kingdom of heaven over marriage as His call for her particular life (see Matthew 19:12).

† Consecrated virgins are women who live married to Jesus in the world as a sign of His deep and particular love for each human soul. Pray for the world's consecrated virgins today and ask God for more women consecrated totally to Him in this way.

DAY 7

Kateri suffered from serious illness during this period. Rather than be discouraged, however, she continued to serve those who were elderly or worse off than she was, and to teach the children their prayers. She was greatly devoted to Jesus in the Blessed Sacrament, often going to Mass both at dawn and at dusk. On Wednesday of Holy Week, 1680, she was taken home to be with Jesus her Bridegroom just before her 24th birthday. Her last words were, "Jesus, Mary, I love you." Fifteen minutes after her death, her smallpox scars disappeared and her face took on an incredibly beautiful appearance.

† By this miracle, God caused the beauty of Kateri's soul to shine through her body. This is what will happen for all of us who, having received baptism and persevered in a state of grace, are resurrected at the Second Coming to join Jesus forever in heaven. Do you pay as much attention to the beauty of your soul as to the beauty of your body?

St. Mary Magdalene

Apostle to the Apostles

Patron saint of women, converts, repentant sinners, contemplatives, pharmacists, those who struggle with sexual temptation, and people ridiculed for their piety, among many others

FEAST DAY: July 22

DAY 1

Mary Magdalene is one of the greatest saints who ever lived. The great theologian St. Thomas Aquinas calls her the Apostle to the Apostles (Latin: *Apostola Apostolorum*) because Jesus entrusted to her the mission of telling the Apostles the good news of the resurrection. Of all of the people in history, Jesus chose Mary to be the first evangelist because of her deep love. When everyone else had gone home saddened, confused, or with a muddled initial faith in the resurrection, Mary stood weeping outside of Jesus's empty tomb. Her desire to be with her Lord grew stronger and stronger, and she was rewarded for it with an encounter with Jesus.

† One of Mary's great strengths was that she never hid her emotions, especially her weeping. Are you tempted to hide your emotions, especially the ones you see as "negative"? It's true that vulnerability can hurt. But try to find good friends you can share your sadness with, and above all, always be real with Jesus. Your perseverance and vulnerability will be rewarded with deep intimacy and joy.

DAY 2

"Why are you weeping? Whom do you seek?" Jesus asked. But she didn't yet know that it was Him. "They have taken away my Lord," she said. "Tell me where you have laid him, and I will take him away" (John 20:13, 15). Then Jesus called her by name: "Mary." She exclaimed, "Rabboni!" (Aramaic for "My teacher!"). As St. Gregory the Great said, "the one whom she sought outwardly was the one who inwardly taught her to keep on searching." Then, having found Jesus—or, better, having been found by Jesus—Mary was given her mission: "Go to my brothers," said Jesus, referring to the disciples (John 20:17).

† Jesus called Mary by name. His love is specific and personal. How is your relationship with Jesus? Ask Him to call you by name. Tell Him, "Jesus, I am open. I desire a deep and personal relationship with You." Then sit in silence for five minutes, letting Him touch your soul.

DAY 3

Mary's first encounter with Jesus is not recorded in the Gospels. We only know, from the Gospel accounts of St. Luke and St. Mark, that Mary had been, at one point, possessed by seven demons. Presumably, her exorcism was her first encounter with the Lord. At some point later, St. Gregory the Great recounted that Mary came to Jesus in the house of Simon the Pharisee, and, "standing behind him at his feet, weeping, she began to wet his feet with her tears, and wiped them with the hair of her head, and kissed his feet, and anointed them with the ointment" (Luke 7:38).

† St. Gregory tells us to imitate Mary, this penitent sinner. "Cry all the faults you remember to have committed both in your adolescence and in your youth; wash by your tears the stains of your manners and works. Let us now love the feet of our Redeemer, whom we have despised by sinning." Repent of your sins. Go to confession. Change your life.

DAY 4

Shocked that Jesus would allow a woman who had been a public sinner to anoint Him, Simon the Pharisee questioned Him, and Jesus replied, in part, "Therefore I tell you, her sins, which are many, are forgiven, for she loved much; but he who is forgiven little, loves little" (Luke 7:47). Mary had been forgiven much. Whatever her public sin had been—the Bible doesn't tell us for sure—she was forgiven. Whatever had allowed the seven demons to take possession of her was gone. Her faith had saved her. She could "go in peace" (Luke 7:50).

† Are there any sins you have confessed but are still holding on to? Open your Bible today and read Luke 7:36–50. Ask Jesus for the gift of peace in the forgiveness He has already given you through the sacrament of reconciliation, also known as confession.

DAY 5

It seems that Mary then began to travel with Jesus, because the very next verses in Luke's Gospel account tell us that "soon afterward he went on through cities and villages, preaching and bringing the good news of the Kingdom of God. And the Twelve were with him, and also some women who had been healed of evil spirits and infirmities: *Mary, called Magdalene, from whom seven demons had gone out*, and Joanna, the wife of Chuza, Herod's steward, and Susanna, and many others, who provided for them out of their means" (Luke 8:1–3, emphasis added).

† Forgiveness leads to mission. Part of Mary's mission, along with Joanna's, Susanna's, and that of many others, was to provide physically for Jesus. Which mission(s) has Jesus given you? Resolve today to live it faithfully.

DAY 6

Sometime later, as told in Luke 10, Jesus came to the home of Martha, Mary's sister, who had a great gift for hospitality. While Martha "was distracted with much serving," Mary sat at Jesus's feet, listening to Him as His disciple. Mary's example, Jesus said, shows the "one thing" that's necessary: a relationship with Him. "Mary has chosen the good portion," He said, "which shall not be taken away from her." This is why Mary Magdalene is patron saint of contemplatives—those who devote themselves to deep and intimate prayer. To contemplate is, in essence, to sit at the feet of Jesus, and Mary is a shining example of that loving, contemplative posture.

† Go to your local church or adoration chapel today. If that's not possible, find a quiet place for prayer in your home. Then say to Jesus, "I want to encounter you. I want to choose the one thing necessary. Be with me now, sweet Jesus." Set a timer for five minutes and simply sit in silence with Him.

DAY 7

True love is always compassionate. The word *compassion* means, literally, "to suffer with." Mary's great love is seen in her repentance, her discipleship, her search for Jesus at the tomb, and her presence with Him at His greatest suffering. When the Apostles fled, it was the women—along with John—who came back, who waited in compassion with Jesus at the foot of the cross. In fact, Mary Magdalene is often seen in depictions of the Crucifixion along with the Blessed Mother and St. John. She is the one on her knees at His feet, weeping for Him and, in a sense, with Him.

† This is where a disciple stays—at the feet of the Master. A disciple learns from the Master, lives like the Master, and leads others to the Master. Mary, the healed demoniac and repentant sinner, did all three and became one of the greatest saints to ever live. No matter your past, follow the example of Mary Magdalene and let your future be sanctity!

WEEK 31

St. Martha

Layperson

Patron saint of homemakers, maids, butlers, cooks, dietitians, innkeepers, and travelers, among others

FEAST DAY: July 29

DAY 1

This week, we meet St. Martha, the sister of St. Mary Magdalene. When Jesus visited Martha and Mary, St. Luke notes that it was Martha's house to which He went. Martha, the dutiful hostess, cared generously for Jesus and her other guests. But rather than focusing on Jesus Himself, Martha became "distracted with much serving" (Luke 10:40), and her distraction led to complaining. When she forgot that the most important thing was to be with Jesus, she forgot the reason for her service and became bitter. Her anxiety about many things had distracted her from the one necessary thing.

† What are the things in your life that distract you from your relationships with Jesus and with other people? What can you do to minimize these worries and distractions?

DAY 2

Notice that Jesus did not tell Martha to stop serving. Of course not! Hospitality is a charism (spiritual gift) from God. And everyone needs to eat and drink. Martha's service was good, but it was poisoned by her anxiety. Maybe she thought that it had to be "perfect" and was frustrated that it wasn't. Maybe she had procrastinated and was annoyed with herself for running late. The Bible doesn't tell us why she was upset, only that we should avoid these troublesome thoughts in favor of deep trust in Jesus. "Therefore I tell you," He said, "do not be anxious about your life . . . fear not, little flock, for it is your Father's good pleasure to give you the kingdom" (Luke 12:22, 32).

† Say a prayer today thanking God for those people in your life who, like Martha, have a gift of hospitality. Drop them a thank-you note (or at least a text message) if you can.

DAY 3

Later, in John 11, we learn that Jesus was particularly close friends with Martha, Mary, and their brother, Lazarus. "Jesus loved Martha and her sister [Mary] and Lazarus," the Bible tells us, and He seems to have found their home in Bethany to be a place of rest for Him. In this, Jesus shows us the value of holy friendship. In the words of St. John Chrysostom, "a friend is more to be longed for than the light; I speak of a genuine one. And wonder not: for it were better for us that the sun should be extinguished, than that we should be deprived of friends; better to live in darkness, than to be without friends."

† Carve out some time to spend with your friends this week—the kind of friends who lead you closer to Jesus.

DAY 4

Lazarus got very sick, so Martha and Mary sent for Jesus. When Jesus arrived, Lazarus was already dead and had been in a tomb for four days. Martha, with her customary forthrightness, went out to meet Jesus when she heard that He was nearby, and in this encounter we see Martha's great faith in Jesus's power. "Lord, if you had been here," she said, "my brother would not have died" (John 11:21). In fact, she added that "even now I know that whatever you ask from God, God will give you" (John 11:22).

✝ Do we have that kind of confidence? Do we know that Jesus will give us what is best? Read John 11 today and ask Jesus for faith like Martha's.

DAY 5

Martha was confident that Lazarus was among the righteous who will rise in the world to come, but Jesus showed her that He Himself is the resurrection and the life. "Do you believe this?" He asked. Martha replied, "Yes, Lord; I believe that you are the Christ, the Son of God, he who is coming into the world" (John 11:25, 27). Even before the resurrection, Martha gave one of the highest expressions of faith in all of the Gospels. Though she was sometimes anxious, troubled, and distracted, she showed an amazing depth of faith.

✝ When we struggle with some trouble or doubt, it's easy for us to think that we've lost faith, are bad Christians, or are otherwise doing something wrong. Usually, though, we've just hit a little bump in the road. We still have faith—it's just a little harder for a while. When you struggle with a time of anxiety, trouble, or distraction, say out loud with Martha, "Yes, Lord, I believe that you are the Christ."

DAY 6

Yet Martha did not completely understand. She called her sister, everyone went out to Lazarus's tomb, and Jesus commanded that the stone be rolled away from its entrance. But Martha protested, "There will be a stench." Jesus replied, "Did I not tell you that if you would believe you would see the glory of God?" and proceeded to raise Lazarus from the dead (John 11:28–44).

† The times when we think that we have it all together or that our faith is perfect are usually the times when we're about to stumble. The gift of humility helps us always look for the glory of God, knowing that we are dependent on Him and are not yet perfected. Turn to page 217 and pray the Litany of Humility today.

DAY 7

We meet Martha by name for the last time in the Gospels during Holy Week, when Jesus, just before His passion, crucifixion, and resurrection, chose to spend His nights with His friends at their home in the town of Bethany, two miles outside of Jerusalem. During that time, they held a dinner for Him, at which Martha served and Mary, for the second time, anointed the feet of Jesus, wiping them with her hair. This time, there was no need for Jesus to rebuke Martha. She still served, but seemingly without anxiety or trouble. It appears as though Martha, the forthright and faithful disciple, had learned the lesson of her Lord.

† In her time with Jesus, Martha had grown. Think about what your life looked like when you first fell in love with Jesus. How are you different today? How have you grown?

WEEK 32

St. Ignatius of Loyola

Priest

Patron saint of soldiers, the Society of Jesus, spiritual directors, and those on retreat

FEAST DAY: July 31

DAY 1

In the lives of other saints, we have already encountered the Society of Jesus, commonly called the Jesuits. This week, we meet its founder, St. Ignatius of Loyola. Born to a Christian family in Azpeitia, Spain, Ignatius always had the heart of a knight. He was fascinated by tales of valor and chivalry, joining the army as soon as he was able. Though he was afflicted by the sin of vainglory (similar to pride and vanity), Ignatius didn't fall prey to many vices common to soldiers. He managed his money well, showed real generosity, and was a peacemaker among his fellow soldiers. But his pride was fierce!

† Every person has a "predominant fault," a vice or sin they struggle with more than other vices. Pay attention this week to how Ignatius conquered his vainglory and ask the Holy Spirit, "Show me my predominant fault and teach me how to conquer it."

DAY 2

Once, at a battle in the city of Pamplona, Ignatius singlehandedly roused the Spanish forces to make a last stand against the overwhelming might of the attacking French army. With his sword drawn, he personally led the last stand until, in the thick of the fight, his right leg was hit by a cannonball and he fell. With Ignatius's fall, the garrison surrendered. Impressed by his courage, the French carried him to the nearby castle of Loyola.

† Our predominant faults are often the "shadow side" of our greatest gifts. We see that in Ignatius's courage and zeal. Ask the Holy Spirit not only to reveal your predominant fault but also to reveal your great gifts.

DAY 3

In Loyola, Ignatius's broken leg was set, but he nearly died in the process. He received the last rites on June 28, the eve of the Solemnity of St. Peter and St. Paul. He had always been devoted to St. Peter, and he prayed earnestly to be saved from death. That night, Ignatius had a dream that Peter touched him and healed him—not so different from what Peter had once done on earth (see Acts 3:1–10). He awoke the next morning free from danger. Despite the miracle, Ignatius held strongly to his vanity. The end of his leg bone stuck out oddly after the break was set. Ignatius, with no anesthesia, had the doctors saw off part of the protruding bone so that he could look more attractive. While that solved one problem, his right leg remained shorter than his left—a problem no surgery could correct—and he walked with a limp for the rest of his life.

† We are all given "thorns in the flesh" (2 Corinthians 12:7), which are actually gifts to help us against our predominant faults. Ignatius's limp, though it may have been annoying, helped him overcome his vainglory. What are some difficulties in your life that have helped you overcome your predominant fault? Thank God for the gift of those difficulties.

DAY 4

Although St. Peter had brought him out of mortal danger, Ignatius remained confined to his bed while his knee healed. Bored, he asked for books about knights and chivalry, but there were none in the castle. Instead, he was given books about Christ and the saints. As he read about the saints, his imagination was captured by their alone time with God, their love of the cross, and their dedication in preaching about Jesus. He found that his thoughts of living a saintly life left him feeling consoled, peaceful, and light, whereas his thoughts of fame, glory, and worldly honor left him feeling heavy, a little sad, and unfulfilled. He decided to devote his life to becoming a saint himself and began to repent, pray, and fast as his recovering body allowed.

† Choose to fill your mind with things that bring consolation, peace, and light while avoiding things that bring heaviness, sadness, and lack of fulfillment.

DAY 5

When he had recovered, Ignatius journeyed to the Benedictine monastery of Montserrat, where he confessed all the sins of his entire life and made a vow of chastity. He left his sword next to the altar and continued to a village called Manresa, where he joyfully did very severe penance. But, becoming overzealous, he did serious harm to his health and landed in a hospital. Although he had been filled with peaceful and joyous consolations since his conversion, Ignatius now fell into much sad, fearful desolation. He had pushed himself too hard, harming his body and his spirit. After a while, under the care of the Dominican priests and brothers at Manresa, he began to eat regularly, live a life of difficult but reasonable penance, and once again receive consolations from God.

† Each Christian should do some fasting and penance in imitation of Jesus's fasting and suffering, but we shouldn't do too much. Commit to some penance (skipping meat on Fridays is a great one!), but, before you start, run it by a wise, spiritual person in your life to make sure it's neither too little nor too much.

DAY 6

In Manresa, Ignatius wrote his *Spiritual Exercises*, which included some advice that's still relevant for us today: "It is one of the devil's artifices to set before a soul some state, holy indeed, but impossible to her, or at least different from hers; that by this love of novelty, she may dislike or be slack in her present state, in which God hath placed her, and which is best for her. In like manner he represents to her other actions as more holy and profitable to make her conceive a disgust of her present employment." In other words, we are meant to become saints exactly where we are—not by daydreaming about going off to do great things but by faithfully doing the little things and receiving any big things that come.

† Another way to say this is "Bloom where you're planted." May we, like Ignatius, find joy, fulfillment, and holiness in the simple, normal day-to-day of our lives.

DAY 7

After traveling to Jerusalem, Ignatius returned to Europe, where he pursued ordination to the priesthood. He began to learn Latin in Barcelona—a 33-year-old man studying alongside young schoolboys. It must have been hard on Ignatius's pride as the boys taunted him for his struggles! But as he continued in his studies, others gathered around him, forming what would become the Society of Jesus. When these companions were eventually ordained as priests, they threw themselves at the feet of the pope, offering themselves for whatever work he thought they should do. For almost 500 years now, the Society of Jesus (although plagued by many trials) has contributed to the building up of the Church.

† Once again, we see Ignatius's vainglory mortified, this time in his study of Latin. Even though Ignatius had already become very holy, he still experienced troubles and still needed to work against this predominant fault of his. Be patient with yourself. Becoming a saint isn't a onetime event—it's a lifetime of choices with and for Jesus!

WEEK 33

St. Jean Vianney

Priest

Patron saint of all priests, especially priests who hear confessions

FEAST DAY: August 4

DAY 1

After growing up in a poor French family, Jean Vianney worked as a farmhand until age 19, when he started pursuing the vocation of the priesthood. He found the academic preparations for the job exceedingly difficult, especially Latin. While some doubted that he'd be a good fit for the priesthood, a priest named Father Balley saw his potential and always advocated for him.

† Who in your life has seen your potential and been a mentor, support, or encouragement to you? Thank God for them, and, if you can, write them a thank-you note today.

DAY 2

Jean was making some progress in his studies, but they were interrupted when he was drafted into the French war with Spain under the leadership of Napoleon Bonaparte. After dutifully reporting to his assigned regiment, Jean visited the church for prayer on the morning when his regiment was supposed to leave for battle. Returning from the church, he found that his fellow soldiers had already left! After an unexpected turn of events and 14 months as a schoolmaster in the town of Noes, he was relieved of his military obligation through the generosity of his younger brother, who took his place in the military. Jean was never required to actually fight in the war—all because he innocently went to pray beforehand.

† The Bible teaches us that "in everything God works for good with those who love him, who are called according to his purpose" (Romans 8:28). God worked for good even in the adventures and mistakes of Jean's life. How is He working for good in your life?

DAY 3

Returning to his preparations for the priesthood, Jean was sent to the seminary, where he continued to struggle greatly in his studies. He even failed his entrance exams on the first attempt but passed them three months later on his second try. Throughout Jean's many trials in seminary, Father Balley stood by his side, encouraging him and going to bat for him with the seminary professors. Had it not been for Father Balley, Jean may not have been allowed to retake his exam and may have never become a priest. Therefore, when he was ordained a priest in 1815, he was assigned to assist Father Balley.

† Each of us have people in our lives who have stood up for us and spoken up on our behalf. Take some time today to reflect back on your life. Thank God for those people and offer some prayer for them, such as a decade of the rosary.

DAY 4

Three years later, when Father Balley died, Jean was made pastor of his own parish in the small town of Ars. He found that, as a result of the French Revolution, very few people came to church and most were not at all concerned about having a relationship with Jesus Christ. On Sunday, the Lord's Day, most of his flock would spend their time working in the fields or going drinking and dancing in the taverns.

† The faith situation in most of the world today is not much different than it was in 19th-century France. Jean was not deterred. He chose to be faithful to Jesus and to his vocation, even in the midst of an apathetic and disengaged society. May we do the same.

DAY 5

Jean began to work diligently to return his flock to the worship of Christ. First, he focused on his own holiness. He couldn't make saints unless he was first growing toward becoming a saint himself. A Christian doesn't have to be saintly yet, but we do have to be moving in that direction if we want to influence others for good. Second, Jean spent time with his people, talking about their lives and families. Third, he prayed and sacrificed. We have seen this over and over again: The only path to becoming a saint is imitating Jesus, who often "would withdraw to deserted places to pray" (Luke 5:16, NABRE) and who "suffered for you, leaving you an example, that you should follow in his steps" (1 Peter 2:21).

† How are you doing with your daily prayer? Do you take time by yourself each day to pray? If you don't, start with five minutes. If you already do, see if you can add five more minutes to your prayer time.

DAY 6

Another key to Jean's success was that he didn't try to do it alone; he fostered relationships with other people who shared his love for Jesus and his desire for parishioners to live in relationship with Him. He also focused on the liturgy. The Second Vatican Council says that the liturgy, especially the Sunday Mass, is the "source and summit of the Christian life." Jean made the church building beautiful and spent hours preparing his Sunday sermons. Finally, he taught his people to pray. They began to learn about the Bible from his sermons and to meditate. They began to examine their consciences and repent of their sins.

† What do your Sundays look like? Sundays are for rest and worship. Is that what you do on Sundays? Or do you work, stress, and worry? Recommit to Sunday as a day of rest and worship.

DAY 7

These meditations and examinations led to the many hours of confessions for which Jean Vianney is famous. After he had spent nine years vigorously working for souls, people started to seek his holiness and wisdom. His parish began to thrive, and he was able to spend more and more time on the sacrament of reconciliation. By the time he had been the pastor of Ars for 30 years, he was spending more than 12 hours per day in the confessional, receiving penitents from his own parish, elsewhere in France, and even other countries.

† When was the last time you went to confession? All Catholics are required to have Sacramental Confession at least once per year if they have committed any serious sins; however, we are encouraged to receive the sacrament regularly to cleanse us from our venial sins—at least once a year but preferably every month or two.

St. Theresa Benedicta of the Cross

Virgin and martyr

Patron saint of Europe, those who have lost parents, converts from Judaism, and World Youth Day

FEAST DAY: August 9

DAY 1

The youngest of 11 children, Edith Stein was born into a Jewish family in Breslau, Germany, in 1891, on Yom Kippur, the Jewish Day of Atonement. Her father died when she was two, leaving her heroic and devout mother to take care of the family as well as a large timber business. Edith lost her faith as a child and, in her own words, "consciously decided, of my own volition, to give up praying."

† Here's a saint who gave up praying when she was still young and didn't take up prayer again for years. As with many young people today, this wasn't merely a phase for Edith; she truly lapsed into unbelief. Yet she'd eventually return to prayer and come to a faith deeper than she ever had as a child. No matter whether or how many times you've given up, you, too, can return, be led deeper, and become a saint.

DAY 2

In 1913, Edith began studying at the University of Göttingen under the renowned philosopher Edmund Husserl, who would eventually be her director for her doctoral dissertation. Husserl's philosophy unintentionally led many of his students to eventually embrace Christianity, including Edith. In these years, she also met another philosopher, Max Scheler, who introduced her to Catholicism.

† The seeds of the faith were planted in Edith nine years before she became Catholic. She did not become a Christian overnight or because of a single event. If there are people in your life who don't have faith, be patient. Pray for them. Fast for them. Speak gently and respectfully to them about Jesus when you have a chance. And be patient. It is God's work, not ours.

DAY 3

In 1917, Edith earned her doctorate in philosophy. While writing her dissertation, she encountered a woman stopping by the cathedral church to kneel for a brief prayer. She later wrote, "This was something totally new to me. In the synagogues and Protestant churches I had visited, people simply went to the services. Here, however, I saw someone coming straight from the busy marketplace into this empty church, as if she was going to have an intimate conversation. It was something I never forgot."

† Visits to the Blessed Sacrament, even for just five minutes, are some of the most powerful everyday acts of prayer. It is an act of faith to simply swing by the church on the way to the grocery store or the office. Try it sometime. If the doors are locked, sit outside for those five minutes, as close to the Blessed Sacrament as you can be.

DAY 4

While Edith was slowly encountering Christ through various ideas, events, and friendships, she was also advancing her career as a philosopher. Sadly, she encountered much prejudice. Although she was clearly brilliant, she was denied professorships because she was a woman and, later, because of her Jewish ethnicity. Later, she would write about her life in a Jewish family: "We who grew up in Judaism have a duty to bear witness . . . to the young generation who are brought up in racial hatred from early childhood."

✝ It is a great shame that sexism and racism existed a hundred years ago, and an even greater shame that these evils continue to exist today. Today, sincerely ask yourself: Are there any ways in which I unjustly discriminate against people based on race, ethnicity, or sex? How can I change my mind and my actions? Start by praying for those against whom you have these reactions.

DAY 5

On January 1, 1922, the Feast of the Circumcision of the Lord, Edith was baptized. This feast commemorates the day when Jesus became, by law, part of the Old Covenant people, and on this day, Edith became a member of the Body of Christ, the "Israel of God" (Galatians 6:16). Edith wrote of her Jewish heritage and her baptism, "I had given up practising my Jewish religion when I was a 14-year-old girl and did not begin to feel Jewish again until I had returned to God." She was confirmed on the Feast of the Purification of the Blessed Virgin Mary, another holiday celebrating a way the Holy Family followed and fulfilled the Old Law.

✝ Jesus was very clear about His position on the Jewish law of the Old Testament: "Do not think that I have come to abolish the law and the prophets; I have come not to abolish them but to fulfil them" (Matthew 5:17). Offer today the Our Father for our Jewish brothers and sisters to whom God spoke first, that they might come to Jesus.

DAY 6

Whereas Edith's position as a woman and a scholar had been looked down on in secular schools, her great intellect was accepted in the academic circles of the Church. The local Benedictine abbot encouraged her to engage in extensive public speaking. She translated works by St. John Henry Newman and St. Thomas Aquinas and was eventually offered a lectureship at the University of Münster.

† The Church has always seen the life of the mind and science as very important, second only to the life of virtue and holiness. How do you engage your mind? Do you read books, listen to podcasts, or watch videos that nourish your mind and build up your faith? Read, listen to, or watch something that nourishes your mind this week.

DAY 7

When the Nazis came to power in 1933, the time also came for Edith to become a Carmelite nun. "Human activities," she said, "cannot help us, but only the suffering of Christ. It is my desire to share in it." Making this decision, she "did not feel any passionate joy . . . but I felt a profound peace—in the safe haven of God's will." As a nun, she took the name Theresa Benedicta of the Cross. Although her superiors smuggled her out of Germany to a convent in the Netherlands for her safety, the shadow of Nazi persecution reached even there. She was arrested by the Gestapo on August 2, 1942, transported to Auschwitz on August 7, and gained her eternal reward as a martyr for her Christian faith and her Jewish blood on August 9.

† In the midst of great suffering and injustice, Theresa embraced the cross with Jesus, Himself a victim of grave injustice. We should never tolerate systemic injustice, but in this fallen world full of sin, most of us will at some point find ourselves victims of some kind of injustice about which we can do nothing. Will we allow ourselves to become bitter and unforgiving, or will we, like Theresa, face evil with the suffering compassion of Christ crucified?

St. Lawrence

Deacon and martyr

Patron saint of Rome, comedians, archivists, firefighters, and the poor, among others

FEAST DAY: August 10

DAY 1

Lawrence is said to be from Roman Hispania (modern-day Spain). He made his way to Rome, where he was mentored by St. Sixtus, the archdeacon there. When Sixtus became pope in AD 257, he made Lawrence archdeacon in his place. The Church had large sums of money in those days, which was used to provide not only for clergy but also for consecrated widows, consecrated virgins, and poor people. The task of the deacons, given by the Holy Spirit through the Apostles, was to care for the poor (Acts 6:1–7), and the job of the archdeacon was to oversee the Church's treasury and provide for the care of a registry of 1,500 people in need.

† We don't get far in life without other people. Over and over, we see that the saints had mentors who taught them, guided them, and walked with them toward their holy goals. If you don't have a mentor, find one. It could be as easy as looking around at church on Sunday and asking someone who appears to be living a good life to join you for lunch or coffee one day.

DAY 2

In that same year, the Roman Emperor Valerian began a persecution of the Church, commanding all bishops, priests, and deacons to be immediately put to death. The next year, Pope St. Sixtus II was captured and martyred. Lawrence, desiring to give his life as Christ had done, wanted to be martyred along with Sixtus; the deacon who served next to the priest at the altar desired to serve his priest at the altar of martyrdom. Sixtus encouraged Lawrence with these words, recorded in Butler's *Lives of the Saints*: "I do not leave you, my son; but a greater trial and a more glorious victory are reserved for you who are stout and in the vigor of youth. We are spared on account of our weakness and old age. You shall follow me in three days."

† Lawrence connected the sacrifice of the Mass, in which the sacrifice of Christ on Calvary is made present again, with the sacrifice of his life. Do you think of the Mass, the Eucharist, and the cross when your life requires sacrifices? Sunday morning, before you go to church, think of the week's sacrifices. Then, when you get to church, imagine placing them on the altar, at the foot of the cross.

DAY 3

Just before his death, Sixtus commanded Lawrence to immediately give the riches of the Church to the poor without moderation, lest they be stolen by the Roman government. Lawrence sold many of the vessels used for Mass, something unthinkable in normal times! It would be better to use them for the worship of God than for anything else—but better to sell them to help the poor than let them fall into the hands of wicked and greedy men.

† Lawrence's first focus was on the God who became poor for us. Open your Bible today and spend some time with Philippians 2:1–18. Thank God for emptying Himself for us and beg for the grace to imitate Him.

DAY 4

The prefect of Rome (a high-ranking government official) heard of the Church's riches and of Lawrence's responsibility for them as archdeacon. Summoning Lawrence, he said, "I am informed that your priests offer in gold, that the sacred blood is received in silver cups, and that in your nocturnal sacrifices you have wax tapers fixed in golden candlesticks. Bring to light these concealed treasures; the prince has need of them for the maintenance of his forces. I am told that according to your doctrine you must render to Caesar the things that belong to him." Lawrence affirmed the wealth of the Church and asked for some time to gather it together and inventory it.

† The wisdom of the world sees only material needs. "Let the things of God be used to outfit the army!" the prefect was basically saying. But the first thing in human life is the worship of God. How do you spend your money? Is your first consideration to give glory to God, or does something else take first place?

DAY 5

Sixtus had guessed correctly. The Roman officials were after the holy items used in the worship of God at Mass. But thanks to his foresight, those items were already gone. So Lawrence spent three days gathering for the prefect the true treasures of the Church: those 1,500 poor people she supported. On the third day, they met at the church and organized themselves into rows—the blind in one row, the orphans in another, and so on—for the prefect to see. As you can imagine, he was irate.

† The wicked Roman officials completely failed to understand the worship of God, whether at the altar of the church or at the altar of the poor. Read Matthew 25:31–46 and follow the clear instructions of Jesus.

DAY 6

Lawrence said to the prefect, "What are you displeased at? The gold which you so eagerly desire is a vile metal and serves to incite men to all manner of crimes. The light of heaven is the true gold, which these poor objects enjoy . . . Behold in these poor persons the treasures which I promised to show you; to which I will add pearls and precious stones—those widows and consecrated virgins, which are the Church's crown, by which it is pleasing to Christ; it hath no other riches: make use then of them for the advantage of Rome, of the emperor, and yourself." Lawrence knew the true riches of the church are the sacraments and those humble souls (poor or rich) who choose to live totally dependent on God.

† Our Lord tells us we should use our money to "make friends" with the poor, who will then pray for us. Open your Bible today to Luke 16:9–13 and pray to God for the gift of generosity.

DAY 7

Displeased with Lawrence's mockery, the prefect prepared a grill heated by coals and said to Lawrence, "You shall die by inches." Lawrence was tied up and thrown naked on the grill to be roasted alive. Caught up in the love of God, Lawrence rejoiced in the torture and, after a long time, said with a smile, "Turn me over; I'm done on this side." Lawrence died happy, praying for the conversion of the city of Rome. It is said that several Roman senators were so moved by his martyrdom that they became Christians on the spot and carried Lawrence's lifeless body to an honorable burial.

† Much of Lawrence's fame comes from his two great jokes: bringing the riches of the church to the prefect in the form of the poor, and making this quip about being "done" while being roasted alive. The Christian life, even in the midst of much suffering, ought to be filled with joy, which will often be expressed in humor. Joy is a fruit of the Holy Spirit (Galatians 5:22). Ask the Holy Spirit for joy and humor in your life today.

WEEK 36

St. Rose of Lima

Virgin

Patron saint of Latin America, Indigenous Americans, gardeners, florists, embroiderers, those who sew lace, and those who struggle against vanity, among others

FEAST DAY: August 23

DAY 1

Born in 1586 in Lima, Peru, Rose was the first canonized saint born in the Americas. Though named Isabel at birth, she was given the nickname "Rose" from infancy, which she took as her name at confirmation. Taking St. Catherine of Siena as her model, Rose started abstaining from fruit and meat and fasting three days a week during her adolescence. Vanity could have been Rose's predominant fault, like it was for Ignatius, but she worked so hard against it from such a young age that it seems never to have given her any serious trouble.

† Children have an incredible capacity for relationship with God. If there are children in your life, take some time to teach them to pray. It's simple. You go first: "What is something you want to say thank you to Jesus for today? Is there something or someone that you want to ask Jesus to help with today?"

DAY 2

Those who seem to "have it all together" from such a young age, however, can be susceptible to the kind of pride for which Jesus denounced the Pharisees. Rose conquered this temptation, too, by true and consistent obedience to her parents. When her parents fell on hard times financially, they sent Rose to work as a servant, where she spent the days gardening and the nights doing needlework (hence her patronage of embroiderers, gardeners, and florists).

† You may have noticed a common theme in the selection of patron saints. We often ask the saints who did the kinds of things we do to be our patrons. What do you love to do? Do a quick search online for "patron saint of _____" and ask that saint to intercede for you.

DAY 3

Rose seems to have enjoyed the simple life of prayer and work as a servant. Her solitude, however, was interrupted by pressures to marry. She wanted to be married to Jesus, as we have seen with so many holy women who came before her, and like them, she was opposed by her parents. But they eventually relented, and at 20 years old, she officially entered the Third Order of the Dominicans and lived publicly her vow of consecrated virginity.

† We've met in our journey through the lives of the saints many who have been formally consecrated to God—virgins, widows, monks, nuns, friars, deacons, priests, and bishops. Today, it's common to idolize "keeping your options open." This makes a permanent choice of celibacy for the Kingdom (see Matthew 19:10–12) difficult. Pray today for more men and women to be consecrated to God, and pray for those who have already been consecrated to persevere in deep intimacy with Jesus Christ.

DAY 4

Rose's brother helped her build a small room in her family's garden, and Rose spent the bulk of her time in the solitude of either work or prayer. She did exceptional penance in union with Christ crucified, including wearing a small tin crown on her head with little pins on the inside. The little pinpricks during the day would remind her of Jesus's crown of thorns and move her to prayer.

† Rose's penances were extreme. It seems like she had a special charism for penance. But every so often, we should all do things that cause us a little discomfort and remind us of God's love throughout our days. Do something today or tomorrow that will remind you of God. Maybe it's writing a prayer on a sticky note, setting a recurring reminder on your phone, or putting a pebble in your shoe. Whatever it is, don't forget how much God loves you—enough to suffer and die for you!

DAY 5

Despite her many penances and her evidently great holiness, Rose was tormented for more than 10 years by the ridicule of others and by many internal trials, including desolations that made her feel far from God and strong temptations to filthy sins. But these bad times were interspersed with many consolations from Jesus, including extraordinary visions of Himself, during which she seems to have experienced, among other graces, the mystical marriage.

† Rose never gave up. It's easy for us to think that, having given Jesus so much of our lives, our lives should now be easy. But the opposite is true. The whole point of Jesus's coming from heaven to earth was to suffer and die for us. He especially loves those who are, like Rose, gifted with a special share in His sufferings. And while this is difficult, it leads to great joy if we choose to persevere!

DAY 6

Rose experienced illness, too, probably at least partially because of her very extreme penance. She would say to Jesus, "Lord, increase my sufferings, and with them increase thy love in my heart." It is a strange and beautiful thing that the sufferings of our relationships, if we bear them well, increase our love. We see this in the trials of human friendships, the trials of romance, and the trials of our relationship with God. Praise God for sufferings! Praise God for increases in love.

† What is one time when your suffering has brought about an increase in your love—for a friend, for your spouse, or for Jesus? Thank God for that increase in love today.

DAY 7

Rose died on August 24, 1617, at only 31 years old. The leading dignitaries of the city were present for her funeral, as was the archbishop. Many miracles followed her death, but perhaps the most incredible had come around 11 years earlier, when Dutch pirates invaded Lima. The Nashville Dominicans tell us that "[t]he women, children and religious of Lima took refuge in the churches. In the church of Santo Domingo, Rose stirred them all to prayer. It is said that as pirates burst into the church, they were confronted with the terrifying spectacle of a young girl ablaze with light, holding a monstrance with the Blessed Sacrament. They turned away and fled to their ships, which sailed away."

† The saints believe in the power of prayer. They pray with faith and mountains are moved (Matthew 17:20–21). Do we, like Rose, believe God's promises that He will work miracles if we pray in faith?

St. Monica

Widow

Patron saint of married women, women in difficult marriages, victims of adultery or verbal abuse, and relatives in need of conversion, among others

FEAST DAY: August 27

DAY 1

So far, we've seen that many of our saints have Christian mothers and pagan fathers. Monica was one of those holy Christian mothers. Born in what is now known as Algeria in AD 332, around 20 years after Christianity became legal in the Roman Empire, she was instructed in the faith by a maid and tutor employed by her family. She was married young to Patricius, a man who was respected in the city but who was sexually promiscuous and had a violent temper. He ridiculed Monica for praying and taking care of the poor, but he didn't strike her or lash out in anger against her.

† Monica lived in a time when there was not much of a way out for victims of the verbal abuse she suffered. While there are many ways out today, they are not available to everyone. Let us pray today that all victims of spousal abuse might find safety and justice! If there is an abuse shelter near you, perhaps you can volunteer or assist in some way.

DAY 2

Monica endured the injustices of Patricius's ridicule and adultery with patience and silence, always praying and waiting for him to be able to receive correction and instruction. She took the biblical advice of St. Peter, being always prepared "to make a defense . . . for the hope that is in you, yet [to] do it with gentleness and reverence; and [to] keep your conscience clear, so that, when you are abused, those who revile your good behavior in Christ may be put to shame" (1 Peter 3:15–16).

† Are you prepared to show others your great hope in our Lord Jesus? Do you read books, listen to podcasts, or watch shows explaining the faith you profess? If you can give a defense, do you do it gently and reverently, or harshly and combatively? Pick up a book or try a show that will strengthen your spiritual life this week, and pray for the gentleness of the Holy Spirit (see Galatians 5:23–35).

DAY 3

Monica became a spiritual adviser to the women of her city, teaching them how to deal with their husbands' vices. Stuck in a bad situation, Monica could have descended into self-pity and despair. Instead, because she was a self-possessed and strong-willed woman, Monica drew on the difficulties and injustice in her own life to help others in similar situations.

† What experiences from your life, either positive or negative, can you use to help others in similar situations? Don't be afraid to appropriately and compassionately share your experiences.

DAY 4

Monica went to church twice every day for the public prayers and was devoted to the intercession of the saints, often visiting the tombs of the martyrs. Her firstborn son grew up to become St. Augustine, a person of singular intelligence and charm. She wanted him to be baptized as a child, but Patricius refused.

† Monica drew strength from prayer, especially the prayer of the Mass and the hearing of the Bible. Try, like her, to make it to a weekday Mass this week, perhaps early in the morning, in the evening, or on your lunch hour.

DAY 5

Monica's patience, gentleness, and reverence paid off when, a year before his death and near his 60th year, Patricius was baptized. His baptism was no mere external act. Patricius was changed both in his soul and his actions, living a truly chaste and Christian life. The formerly cruel, unbelieving husband was "consecrated through his wife" (1 Corinthians 7:14). Monica's patient, gentle reverence converted not only her husband but also her mother-in-law.

† Is there a time when a long-held prayer of yours was finally answered? Thank God for that answer today.

DAY 6

Two years after Patricius's death, Augustine left the Christian faith in which, though unbaptized, he was a catechumen (someone preparing for baptism). This greatly grieved Monica. Praying fervently for the reversion and baptism of her son, Monica was given a dream in which she was standing on a wooden ruler, very sad. A young man of shining light encouraged her to dry her tears, saying, "Your son is with you." And there was Augustine, standing on the rule of the faith with her. She was comforted by the dream and told Augustine about it. He didn't think he would become a Christian again, but he never forgot the dream. Neither did Monica; she waited nine long years for her son's conversion.

† Even though she received assurance from God that her prayer would be answered, she was not told when. Still, she waited patiently for His timing. May we have patience like Monica!

DAY 7

On Easter 387, Monica's great desire was realized when her son finally received the grace of baptism in Milan, Italy. That year, Monica and Augustine set out to return to their native Africa. She told him, "Son, there is nothing now in this life that affords me any delight . . . The only thing for which I desired to live was that I might see you a Catholic and child of heaven. God has done much more, in that I see you now . . . entirely devoted to his service. What further business then have I here?" Soon after, Monica departed this life to be with the Lord.

† After a life of suffering, Monica died a happy death in the peace of the will of God, seeing the fruit of her years of prayer. Ask God for this grace to die not on our own terms but in His will, which is our peace.

St. Gregory the Great

Pope and Doctor of the Church

Patron saint of musicians, singers, students, and teachers

FEAST DAY: September 3

DAY 1

In the year 540, a son was born to the wealthy Roman senator Gordianus and his wife, Silvia, who, despite their wealth and prestige, were devout and faithful Catholics. That son, Gregory, grew up to become governor and chief judge of the city at the relatively young age of 34. A year or so later, after his father died, Gregory converted seven of the family estates he'd inherited into monasteries and soon became a monk in one of them. He spent three years in the monastery, taking on severe sacrifices and penances. He tells us these years were the happiest of his life.

† Even—perhaps especially—in the midst of political, economic, and moral decline, God raises up great saints who, faithful in the small things of their daily lives, transform the world. Strive to be one of those saints.

DAY 2

Walking through the Roman market one day, Gregory caught sight of young men from Britain being sold as slaves. Seeing them not as property but as human beings called to become sons of God, he asked if the people where they were from were Christians. He learned that the gospel had not yet been preached to them and declared it "a lamentable consideration that the prince of darkness should be master of so much beauty." Although Gregory was not allowed to go immediately to Britain as a missionary, he never forgot the love for the English that God had placed into his heart.

† Do you "see" other people, even if their skin color or socio-economic status is different from yours? Make an effort to take an interest in the lives of people who are different from you.

DAY 3

Soon, Gregory was called on to use his talents of governance and administration for the good of the Church. Although he wanted to remain a monk, the pope ordained him as one of the seven deacons in charge of his own region of Rome, a role his father had once held. And then, to Gregory's further displeasure, the pope sent him on a diplomatic mission to Constantinople that lasted for six years. Although Gregory had no desire to use his talents in this way, he knew that doing so was the will of God, and, in the midst of great challenges, he benefited greatly from his time there.

† What talents do you have? Open your Bible to Matthew 25:14-30 today and ask Jesus, "How are you calling me to use my talents? For my church? For my city? For my family?"

DAY 4

The year 589 was a year of disaster in Rome. Incredible flooding devastated Italy, and a plague followed. In the midst of all of this, Pope Pelagius II died, and Gregory was elected to take his place. With the plague still raging and before he'd officially taken the throne as pope, Gregory organized a procession with seven legs, each beginning in one of the seven regions of the city at the same time and all ending together at the Basilica of St. Mary Major. The plague, it seems, ended shortly thereafter.

✝ Do we believe as strongly as Gregory in the power of prayer? God doesn't always answer our prayers with a yes, but that doesn't mean we shouldn't offer them. Sometimes, our diligent prayer, combined with God's answering no, is actually what helps us grow, develop, and become saints. Never give up on prayer!

DAY 5

When the time came for him to officially become pope, Gregory left the city for three days, hiding in the woods to avoid receiving such a massive responsibility in the midst of such great suffering in the city. As the people of Rome prayed and fasted, they searched for Gregory and, it's said, found him because God miraculously revealed his hiding place. After this clear sign of the will of God, Gregory was unable to resist and became pope on September 3, 590, which is now his feast day.

✝ Gregory made a mistake in discerning God's will. Have you ever been afraid to make a mistake in your discernment? Most of us have. But be not afraid! God wants you to know His will. Keep praying, keep fasting, and He will guide you in the right direction, even if, like Gregory, you make a mistake.

DAY 6

God used even Gregory's humble mistake for the good of future generations of Christians. When John, the archbishop of Ravenna, corrected Gregory for having fled, Gregory wrote a book, known in English as *Pastoral Rule*, in response. It begins with these words to John: "You reprove me, beloved brother, with a kind and humble intention, for having hoped that by hiding myself I might flee the burdens of pastoral care. Now, so that no one may believe that these burdens are light, I write the present book to express my opinion of the severity of their weight so that he who is free of these burdens might not recklessly pursue them and he who has already attained them might tremble for having done so." This work has been a blessing to Christian pastors and their flocks ever since.

† Open your Bible to Romans 8:28 and think about how God brings good even out of our mistakes.

DAY 7

As pope for 14 years, Gregory cared for the physical, spiritual, and political well-being of his people. He was always sure to care well for the poor both in Rome and wherever he had influence. Remembering his encounter with the enslaved people from Britain, he sent missionaries, including St. Augustine of Canterbury, to bring the good news of Jesus to Britain. He established the practice of "station churches," in which, still to this day, the pope goes on a procession to various churches in Rome during Lent to have Mass and preach to his people in person. Finally, with the Roman government disinterested, Gregory was forced into leading diplomatic negotiations with the most significant neighboring powers, the Lombards and the Franks.

† It's common today for pastors to have, like Gregory, all sorts of varied and difficult tasks (though not usually of international consequence). Pray for your pastor every day and seriously consider where you might be able to offer a helping hand.

St. Teresa of Calcutta

Religious sister

Patron saint of World Youth Day, the Missionaries of
Charity, and the Archdiocese of Calcutta

FEAST DAY: September 5

DAY 1

On October 26, 1985, Mother Teresa of Calcutta addressed
the United Nations General Assembly. To introduce her,
Secretary-General Javier Pérez de Cuéllar declared, "I present
to you the most powerful woman in the world." Although she held
no political office, commanded no armies, and had taken a vow
of poverty, this five-foot-tall Catholic nun from Albania was the
most powerful woman in the world. Why? Because she loved.
She chose over and over again, by the grace of God, to care for
those who most needed love. As a result, she wielded more moral
authority with that love than others did with their might.

† Turn to page 217 and pray the Litany of Humility today. Ask
for the grace of humble love like Mother Teresa.

DAY 2

Born Anjezë Gonxhe (in English, "Agnes Little Flower") Bojaxhiu in what is now called North Macedonia, Agnes was fascinated by stories of saintly missionaries. By age 12, she was convinced she should give her life completely to Jesus as a nun. After many spiritual conversations with her mother and her priest, who guided her in this discernment, Agnes left home at 18 years old to join the Sisters of Loreto, where she took the name Teresa. Soon she was sent to Ireland for her formation as a nun and as a missionary.

† God speaks to His children, including those of us who are young. If you're a young person, let these stories of the saints inspire you. Is God saying something to you through their stories? If you're no longer a young person, commit some of these stories to memory and share them with the children and teenagers in your life.

DAY 3

When Agnes asked for her mother's blessing to leave home and be completely devoted to Jesus as a nun, tears welled up in her mother's eyes, and she remained in her room for a day. What was she doing? She was praying. Emerging a day later, she gave Agnes her blessing and reminded her to put her hand to the plow and never look back. After Agnes's departure, they never saw one another again in this life.

† Agnes's mother remembered the words of Jesus and encouraged her daughter to be totally devoted to Him. Open your Bible to Luke 9:57-62 and ask Mother Teresa to pray for you that you might be totally devoted to Jesus.

DAY 4

After learning English in Ireland and receiving further formation in the Indian city of Darjeeling, Teresa spent around 20 years as a teacher in Calcutta, where she saw firsthand great suffering and poverty in the streets around her. On September 10, 1946, Teresa was traveling by train with one of her sisters when she received what she termed her "call within a call" to "leave the convent and help the poor while living among them. It was an order [from Jesus]." From that point, she began to experience in various ways the thirst of Christ crucified.

† Open your Bible to John 19:25-30 today. Ask Jesus to show you His thirst: His thirst for the poor, for the salvation of the world, for your love.

DAY 5

Teresa received permission to leave the Sisters of Loreto and begin working among the poor in 1948. Taking off the habit of Loreto, she adopted as her habit a traditional Indian garment: the cotton sari in which she is usually depicted. She was determined to live in poverty, with the poor and for the poor. In 1949, she got permission to receive other women, some of them her former students, to join her in her mission, and in 1950, what would become the Missionaries of Charity became a diocesan religious congregation.

† It's easier to pity others than to share in their experience. God may not be calling you to move out of your house like Mother Teresa, but how can you go a little out of your way to share in the experiences of someone else, especially someone different from you?

DAY 6

Amid much suffering and slander, the Missionaries of Charity flourished with the simple mission of satisfying the thirst of Jesus through prayer and service. The dying, the lepers, the orphans, and others who suffer were all cared for by the sisters, whose number rapidly grew. Poor Hindus, poor Muslims, poor Christians, and all others were served, loved, and respected by the sisters, who desired only to express to everyone the love of Jesus their Bridegroom. As Teresa said, "By blood, I am Albanian. By citizenship, an Indian. By faith, I am a Catholic nun. As to my calling, I belong to the world. As to my heart, I belong entirely to the heart of Jesus."

† Mother Teresa's energy and conviction came from her daily visits to Jesus in the Blessed Sacrament. Visit Jesus in your local church or adoration chapel if you can today and beg for the grace to show His love to the people you encounter.

DAY 7

Mother Teresa's great service to humanity was recognized by people of all nations, faiths, cultures, and political parties. She was awarded the Nobel Peace Prize in 1979, along with many other civic honors (including honorary US citizenship). In 2012, the United Nations General Assembly designated September 5, the day of her death, as the International Day of Charity in her honor. It's fitting to end our conversation about this great saint with Pope Francis's words at her canonization: "May this tireless worker of mercy help us increasingly to understand that our only criterion for action is gratuitous love, free from every ideology and all obligations, offered freely to everyone without distinction of language, culture, race or religion."

† Words from Pope Francis's homily can also serve as our call to action today: "Mother Teresa loved to say, 'Perhaps I don't speak their language, but I can smile.' Let us carry her smile in our hearts and give it to those whom we meet along our journey, especially those who suffer."

St. Helena

Empress

Patron saint of archaeologists, converts, difficult marriages, divorced people, and empresses

FEAST DAY: August 18 (but intimately connected to the Feast of the Exaltation of the Holy Cross on September 14)

DAY 1

In the hundred years following the passion and resurrection of Jesus, there was much strife between the Jews and the Romans. In AD 70, the First Roman-Jewish War resulted in the destruction of the temple in Jerusalem, as Jesus had predicted. Then, in 132, another Jewish rebellion began, led by Simon bar Kokhba. By the end, the Jews were utterly defeated. In an effort to wipe Judaism from the land, Emperor Hadrian erected pagan temples over Jewish and Christian holy sites, including the location of Jesus's crucifixion, burial, and resurrection. Ironically, Hadrian's destruction was used by God to preserve the location of these holy sites until, almost 200 years later, Christianity became legal in the empire.

† We repeat this lesson often because it is so important. Open your Bible to Romans 8:28 and thank God for all of the ways He works things for the good in your life.

DAY 2

Helena was born about 120 years after Hadrian's destruction of holy sites. She was probably from Britain, although not everyone agrees about that. We do know that she married Constantius, a member of the Roman army, and soon their eldest son was born: Constantine, who would become the great emperor of Rome. In pursuit of political power, however, Constantius divorced Helena to marry Theodora, an emperor's daughter-in-law. This is why Helena is a patron saint of divorced people.

† Domestic troubles are hard: to be divorced for political gain, to be put second to work, pleasure, or something else. Maybe you know this from experience. Open your Bible to Isaiah 43:1–7, asking Helena to pray with you and for you.

DAY 3

Helena, unlike many of our saints, was not born into a Christian family, and while she seems to have had some interest in and empathy for Christians, she did not become one until after Jesus helped her son, Constantine, defeat the wicked Emperor Maxentius in 312. She was likely over 60 years old at the time of her conversion. Although her son gave her the highest titles in the empire and even had medals made with her image, Helena kept a humble servant's heart. She attended daily prayers and Masses, served the poor, and, though she dressed in simple clothing, adorned the churches with gold, silver, and jewels.

† Have you ever thought, "I'm too old for that" or "It's too late for me"? Be assured that you're not too old. It's not too late. So long as there is breath in your lungs and a beat in your heart, you can become a saint. Whether old or young, follow the example of Helena!

DAY 4

In 324, Constantine became sole emperor of Rome. Two years later, Helena journeyed to Jerusalem to visit the places made holy by God's physical presence. Inflamed with a great desire to find the True Cross on which our Savior died, Helena did her research and learned that crosses were customarily buried close to the place of crucifixion. Having the temple of Venus removed by her authority as empress, she found the Holy Sepulcher (the place of Jesus's burial), three buried crosses, nails, and the placard that read "Jesus of Nazareth, King of the Jews" (see John 19:20).

✝ Helena was inspired to do a good thing for God—uncovering all of these holy sites so they could be used again for worship. What sets your heart on fire? What might you like to do for God? Take the first step.

DAY 5

Which of the three buried crosses had belonged to Jesus? Since the placard was separate from the crosses, Helena had no human way to find out which cross was for Jesus. She consulted the bishop St. Macarius, who suggested that all three crosses be brought to a lady in Jerusalem who was very ill. Praying, they touched the first two to her body with no effect. With the touch of the third cross, however, the woman was miraculously cured. This was the True Cross that had touched the flesh of the Savior, absorbing the blood of His grievous wounds and by which He saved the world!

✝ Whenever God works a miracle, there is a reason or a lesson. If every request were granted and physical miracles were common, then they wouldn't be miracles. Most of the time, being with Jesus in the day-to-day joys and suffering of our lives is where our true peace is found. His incarnation and crucifixion show us how much He loves us in our normal human lives.

DAY 6

Having found the True Cross, Helena had a church built over the Holy Sepulcher and Calvary. One third of the cross was kept there, another third was carried to her son, Emperor Constantine, and the last third went to Rome, where it is now housed along with the placard in the Church of the Holy Cross (*Santa Croce*), encased in fine reliquaries to show the value of our salvation in Christ. Upon delivering these relics, Helena died in her son's arms on August 18, in either 326 or 328. Since then, tiny splinters of the cross have been sent around the world so that all peoples might see and venerate the cross on which our Savior died.

† Research if there are any relics of the True Cross in churches near where you live. (Start with parishes named Holy Cross.) Make a little pilgrimage to pray to Jesus before His cross if you can.

DAY 7

How did Jesus conquer sin and death and Satan and hell? By His sacrifice on the cross! The cross, St. Paul wrote, is "the power of God" for those being saved (1 Corinthians 1:18). The middle of September brings us to a great but often unknown feast of the year: the Feast of the Exaltation of the Holy Cross. On this day, we celebrate the power of Christ overcoming the wickedness of the devil.

† Every Good Friday, we kiss the wood of the cross in gratitude for Jesus's great sacrifice for us. Do you have a cross or a crucifix in your home? Around your neck? Kiss it today in gratitude.

St. Hildegard of Bingen

Virgin, abbess, and Doctor of the Church

Patron saint of scientists, biologists, musicians, and writers

FEAST DAY: September 17

DAY 1

St. Hildegard was an amazingly intelligent person. Making significant contributions in biology, music, and theology, she is one of the four female Doctors of the Church—that is, saints declared by the Catholic Church to be particularly excellent teachers of sacred theology. From a young age, she experienced visions from God. She described one in which her soul "rises up high into the vault of heaven and into the changing sky and spreads itself out among different peoples, although they are far away from me in distant lands and places." These visions, however, also came with the sufferings of Christ, especially in the form of headaches.

† What a grace that Jesus gives, even to the very young! Offer some prayer today, perhaps a rosary, that young people might generously receive the love of God.

DAY 2

As was common in the Middle Ages, Hildegard was sent as an oblate to the monastery, beginning, it seems, around adolescence. There she was mentored by Jutta, a nun six years older than she was. She was taught to read and sing the Psalms in Latin, as the nuns prayed together each day. She never learned to write proficiently, however. Jutta became superior of the convent, and after her young death, Hildegard was unanimously elected as her successor.

† Despite Hildegard's clear blessings from God, she did not try to live as a Christian on her own. Even someone as gifted as Hildegard needed a mentor. Identify people you admire and seek their advice. Ask something like, "What do you do that keeps you so disciplined/prayerful/humble/etc.?"

DAY 3

When he proclaimed her as a Doctor of the Church, Pope Benedict XVI said, "In Saint Hildegard of Bingen there is a wonderful harmony between teaching and daily life. In her, the search for God's will in the imitation of Christ was expressed in the constant practice of virtue, which she exercised with supreme generosity and which she nourished from biblical, liturgical and patristic roots in the light of the Rule of Saint Benedict. Her persevering practice of obedience, simplicity, charity and hospitality was especially visible. In her desire to belong completely to the Lord, this Benedictine Abbess was able to bring together rare human gifts, keen intelligence and an ability to penetrate heavenly realities."

† Put simply, Hildegard took her natural talents, which were many, and used them for love of God and neighbor. May we do the same!

DAY 4

Hildegard's knowledge, holiness, and goodness were so recognized in Europe that the pope himself asked her to travel and to preach so others could drink from the fountain of Christ, the Teacher who had so enlightened her. She was given by God a "shadow of living light" in which she saw reality, in a sense, with God's eyes. He gave Hildegard a lifetime of mystical visions—and the sufferings that come with them—because of His simple love for her and so that they could be shared with others.

† We each want to make our impact on the world. That desire is good, and we'll only fulfill it by sharing the particular gifts God gave each of us. Maybe your gift is quiet service. Then quietly serve. Maybe your gift is teaching. Then teach. Whatever your gifts, they are for you and for the world.

DAY 5

Hildegard was a great composer of music, especially liturgical music for women's voices. She taught that human singing, especially in liturgical worship, is the response of humankind to God, who speaks first. A human person responds to God in two ways: "in the voice of prayer" (i.e., liturgical worship), and "in the voice of heart" (i.e., a life of holiness and virtue). The whole human life, therefore—in addition to the physical act of singing—is called to be a "harmonic and symphonic" response to God.

† Listen to some of Hildegard's music today; a quick search online will turn up plenty. Then, when you go to church this Sunday, sing. Let the sound from your throat express the harmony of your life and join with the angels in praise of God!

DAY 6

Hildegard was determined to do the right thing, no matter the cost. In the last year of her life, a young man who had been excommunicated (formally removed from the Church) was buried in her convent's cemetery. Although the man had been reconciled to the Church on his deathbed, receiving the last sacraments, the archbishop of Mainz insisted that his body be exhumed and buried in some other place. Hildegard, knowing that the last rites had reconciled this man with God and His Church, refused, noting that the archbishop's actions were due to stubbornness and pride. He punished her monastery with the removal of the sacraments (called "interdict"), which was only lifted upon his death.

† Hildegard was willing to stand up even to the archbishop, enduring and fighting against unjust punishment even when it was difficult and painful. Where do you see injustice in the world? Where do people in your life speak poorly or do wrong to others? Do you say something? Do you stand up for those unjustly oppressed?

DAY 7

Hildegard's writings were not limited to theology and music. She also wrote extensively on the natural sciences, especially medicine and herbology; catalogued the properties of various animals, plants, and stones; and wrote about the constitution of the human body and how to heal it from various diseases. She saw in the Bible, especially the book of Genesis, the goodness of God's creation, which, although fallen because of sin, remains good.

† Open your Bible today and read Genesis 1:1–2:3. Thank God for all the good things of the earth and think about how you might enjoy them. Maybe it would be good to go for a walk as part of your prayer today.

St. Matthew

Apostle and evangelist

Patron saint of accountants, bankers, tax collectors, civil servants, and perfumers

FEAST DAY: September 21

DAY 1

Matthew, whose other name was Levi, was a tax collector in the city of Capernaum, which had become Jesus's base of operations, so to speak, after He began His public ministry. In his Gospel, Matthew wrote of his own call to become a disciple in the simplest of terms. "As Jesus passed on from there, he saw a man called Matthew sitting at the tax office; and he said to him, 'Follow me.' And he rose and followed him" (Matthew 9:1). St. Luke tells us Matthew then held a feast at his house, inviting "a large company of tax collectors and others" (Luke 5:29). Right after becoming a disciple, Matthew introduced others to Jesus.

† While it's true that we need mentoring, study, and training as disciples, we can't wait for that before we begin simply telling other people what Jesus has done for us. All Matthew did, in these first moments of his discipleship, was introduce people to Jesus. May we do the same, no matter whether we are beginners or advanced.

DAY 2

Matthew was a tax collector. What does that mean? He was a Jew *and* an employee of the powerful Roman Empire that occupied and oppressed the Jews. He was seen as a traitor by his own people. Not only that, but tax collectors were known for collecting more money than was due and skimming off the top. It must have seemed shocking that Jesus would call someone like this!

† Have you ever been shocked by a conversion in someone's life? Do you struggle to believe it? Commit yourself today to seeking out those people whose conversions came as a shock to others and offering them some appropriate encouragement.

DAY 3

Our friend St. Bede says that Jesus "saw [Matthew] through the eyes of mercy and chose him." Matthew was chosen as a disciple not because Jesus saw his virtue, his efforts, or even his potential. Matthew was chosen because Jesus had mercy upon him. Matthew was probably not very different from some people in business today. "I can take a little off the top here, right?" "Cheating on my taxes isn't that bad." "My boss won't miss it if I take this thing from the office."

† Jesus isn't pleased with these dishonesties in our lives, but He looks on us with eyes of mercy and calls each of us into deep, abiding relationship with Himself. Ask yourself: How can I be more honest in my profession and in my daily life?

DAY 4

The Bible tells us that on one occasion, Jesus went up into the hills and prayed all night to the Father. Then "he appointed twelve" of his disciples for three tasks: to *be with Him,* to preach, and to cast out demons. Matthew was one of the Twelve called to be intimate companions of Jesus—truly His friends.

† In our focus on this or that mission Jesus is calling us to, it's easy to forget that the first thing He wants from and for us is to simply be with Him. Read Mark 3:13–19, then take five minutes in silence to simply be with Jesus.

DAY 5

When they write about Matthew's former work as a (presumably dishonest) tax collector, St. Mark and St. Luke use the name Levi. St. Jerome and St. John Chrysostom tell us that they do so out of reverence for his conversion: Matthew is not the same man he was before that, and it's unjust for human beings to hold past sins against someone whom God has forgiven. But when Matthew refers to himself, he openly uses the name by which he is known as a Christian, humbly showing the whole world what God can do in the life of a sinner.

† Following the example of Mark and Luke, we should be careful when talking about the past sins of a fellow Christian who has repented. Matthew's example, on the other hand, shows us that we should humbly admit our own past sins to give glory to God for the great work of conversion that He has accomplished in us.

DAY 6

After Jesus's ascension, Matthew preached for a while in the Holy Land, most likely writing his Gospel in Hebrew or Aramaic. Sometime later, after St. Mark wrote his Gospel, it seems as though Matthew's writing was translated into Greek and edited based on Mark's to form the Gospel of Matthew as we have it today. St. Bartholomew is said to have taken a copy with him to India and left it there.

† Being trained in reading and writing (uncommon skills back then), Matthew used his talents to preach the gospel. What talents and platforms do you have to preach the gospel? In your workplace? In your family? On social media?

DAY 7

Matthew proclaimed the gospel not only through the written word but also through his life. After preaching in Judea, he went to the East, most likely the northern part of modern-day Iran. He's believed to have lived like a monk, with constant prayer and frequent fasting interrupted only to proclaim the gospel, and to have died a martyr.

† Matthew is one of the most famous Christians in history, but his life after the ascension of our Lord seems to have been very simple. He prayed, he fasted, and he preached. He was courageous enough to preach even when there was opposition, choosing to follow Jesus even to the point of shedding his blood. May we live the same kind of clear, simple, focused lives.

St. Michael, St. Gabriel & St. Raphael

Archangels

Patron saints of soldiers, police officers, physicians, messengers, travelers, and those searching for a spouse

FEAST DAY: September 29

DAY 1

This week brings us to a different kind of saint as we turn our attention to the holy archangels. You might be asking: Why are these angels called "saints"? Are angels and saints the same thing? No. Angels are pure spirits, while humans are both soul and body united together. But an angel is a person, and a human is also a person. And each angel, similar to each human, had an opportunity to live for God or to live against God. The two-thirds of these spirits who chose to live for Him are called angels, and the one-third who chose to live against Him are called demons (see Revelation 12:4).

† It's easy to find ourselves afraid of demons, but there is great comfort in knowing that there are twice as many holy angels as there are demons. Turn to page 219 and pray the Prayer to St. Michael today.

DAY 2

Showing our friendship with the holy angels, the Church has instituted feast days for all of the angels specifically mentioned in the Bible. On September 29, we celebrate the three archangels named in Scripture, and on October 2, we celebrate the guardian angel assigned to each of us (mentioned by Jesus in Matthew 18:10). An archangel is an angel of particular power and dignity. Knowing that a saint is more or less a person in heaven, and seeing these particular personal, spiritual beings in the Bible, the Church celebrates them and asks for their help along with the human saints.

† With gratitude to God for your guardian angel, read Matthew 18:10 in your Bible today. Then turn to page 219 and pray the Guardian Angel Prayer.

DAY 3

The name Michael is Hebrew for "Who is like God?" Ancient Christians teach us that the words in Isaiah 14:13–14 are Satan's: "I will ascend to heaven; above the stars [angels] of God. . . . I will make myself like the Most High." It's said that Michael's response to this is his name: "Who is like God?" Michael's humility is contrasted with Lucifer's pride. When war arose in heaven, "Michael and his angels [were] fighting against the dragon; and the dragon and his angels . . . were defeated and there was no longer any place for them in heaven. And the great dragon was thrown down, that ancient serpent, who is called the Devil and Satan, the deceiver of the whole world—he was thrown down to the earth, and his angels were thrown down with him" (Revelation 12:7–9).

† Beg Jesus for humility like St. Michael's today. Turn to page 217 and pray the Litany of Humility.

DAY 4

Based on Scripture (Daniel 10, Daniel 12, Jude, and Revelation 12:7–9), Christian tradition holds that St. Michael has four offices or duties: fighting against Satan, rescuing faithful Christian souls from Satan's power (especially near death), defending God's people, and guiding souls from the earth to stand before the judgment seat of God.

† God loves you so much that He employs these powerful spiritual beings to care for, protect, and guide you. Say this prayer today, giving glory to the Holy Trinity for sending us such great helpers: "Glory be to the Father and to the Son and to the Holy Spirit. As it was in the beginning, is now, and ever shall be, world without end. Amen."

DAY 5

The name Gabriel means "strength of God." In the book of Daniel in the Old Testament, Gabriel comes to announce prophecies of the future, including the one about when the Messiah will be born. Then, hundreds of years later, as God's people wait with expectant hope for the coming of Jesus the Messiah, Gabriel appears again—first to Zechariah to announce the conception and birth of John the Baptist, then to Mary to announce the birth of Jesus, the Messiah and Son of God.

† Gabriel appears to humble servants of God to announce the hidden but powerful work of God, who casts down the mighty from their thrones and lifts up the lowly. Open your Bible today and meditate on Mary's words in Luke 1:46-55.

DAY 6

We meet Raphael, whose name means "healing of God," in the Old Testament book of Tobit. Many miles apart, a man named Tobit and a woman named Sarah both prayed to God. Tobit, an old man, and Sarah, a young woman, each in the midst of deep suffering, both prayed for death. "At that very moment, the prayer of both was heard in the presence of the glory of the great God. And Raphael was sent to heal the two of them" (Tobit 3:16–17).

† How many angels, how many human saints, and how many people on earth accompany us along our pilgrimage! Take some time today to think of your guardian angel, your patron saints, and the people in your life who guide you to the Lord. End with a small prayer of thanksgiving to God for them.

DAY 7

There are nine types of angels mentioned in the Bible, which saints and theologians have traditionally ordered into "choirs." Why would we call the divisions of angels "choirs"? Maybe because they sing God's praises in the heavenly liturgy. In the book of Isaiah, for example, we meet the seraphim, who sing out the words we sing at Mass just before the Consecration: "Holy, holy, holy is the Lord of hosts" (Isaiah 6:3). The angels have many tasks, but singing God's praises is their primary role. As Christians, that's our primary task, too: to give glory to God with every breath of our lips and every action of our lives.

† When you go to church this weekend, sing, even if you can't sing well. Sing in union with the angels, giving to God the praise that is His due.

St. Thérèse of Lisieux

Virgin and Doctor of the Church

Patron saint of France, the gardens of Vatican City, florists, gardeners, missionaries, those who have lost parents, and those who suffer from tuberculosis

FEAST DAY: October 1

DAY 1

Thérèse, born Marie Françoise-Thérèse Martin on January 2, 1873, was called by Pope St. Pius X "the greatest saint of modern times." Her parents, Louis and Zélie, were incredibly holy, as were her sisters. The Martin family attended Mass at 5:30 a.m. daily, practiced fasting, and prayed as a family regularly. They visited the sick and the elderly and cared for the poor. Thérèse and her four sisters all became nuns; Louis and Zélie were canonized as saints in 2015.

† We meet in the Martins another family of great holiness. Ask St. Louis and St. Zélie to pray for you and your spouse today. Or, if you're unmarried, ask them to pray with you for a married couple you know.

DAY 2

As a baby, Thérèse was so frail that it was unclear whether she would survive. She recovered, thanks be to God, but she suffered with poor health on and off throughout her life. Being the youngest and so sickly, Thérèse was probably a bit spoiled. She certainly had a temper and a tendency to overreact. Her greatest childhood struggle, however, was the untimely death of her mother, Zélie, who died of breast cancer in 1877 when Thérèse was only four years old. For 10 years, she seems to have struggled with intense emotional pain and anxiety, which may have exacerbated or even caused some of her physical illnesses.

† Do you struggle with a temper or with being unreasonably upset when things don't go your way? Thérèse did, too. Never take it out on others who are innocent. Instead, do as Thérèse did and bring your anger or distress to Jesus with raw honesty.

DAY 3

When Thérèse was 10, she fell seriously ill again. This time, on Pentecost in 1883, she received a miraculous healing. Masses arranged by her father were being prayed for her in Paris, and Thérèse's sisters were praying with her in her room, asking for the Blessed Virgin Mary to help. Suddenly, as Thérèse described it, the room's statue of the "Blessed Virgin glowed with a beauty beyond anything I had ever seen. Her face was alive with kindness and an infinite tenderness, but it was her enchanting smile which really moved me to the depths. My pain vanished and two great tears crept down my cheeks—tears of pure joy. 'Oh,' I thought, 'how happy I am that the Blessed Virgin has smiled at me.'" Thérèse's body was miraculously cured.

† How God delights to answer our prayers! Offer a decade of the rosary for the sick today.

DAY 4

On Christmas Day in 1886, Thérèse experienced what she called "the grace of emerging from childhood—the grace of my complete conversion," when God healed her from what she calls her "extreme sensitivities [that] made me quite unendurable." She still delighted in the children's Christmas tradition of having her shoes filled with presents near the fireplace, and when she overheard her father expressing excitement that this would be the last year of this childish tradition, Thérèse was very hurt. But this time, she didn't descend into tears and outbursts. Instead, though she was certainly still hurt and retained the gift of her sensitivity, she was now able to live with it. "Love filled my heart," she wrote. "I forgot myself and henceforth I was happy."

† Do you struggle with anxiety or "extreme sensitivities"? If so, ask Thérèse to pray for you. Boldly ask Jesus to grant you a miracle like He granted her!

DAY 5

One reason that Thérèse begged Jesus so earnestly for this healing was because she desired to be a Carmelite nun. She first sought to join the order at 15 years old, but she was too young. Over and over again, she was denied entrance into the convent. "The nearer I got to my goal," she wrote, "the more difficulties there were."

† Each of our lives is filled with difficulties. Thérèse's short life was filled with many, yet she became "the greatest saint of modern times." Why? How? By always honestly going to Jesus with her difficulties and her pain. Do you talk to Jesus when you're hurting, or do you isolate yourself from Him? Always be honest in prayer. Always be raw. Jesus loves you and can see through your masks.

DAY 6

On November 20, 1887, many people from the Diocese of Lisieux were in Rome before Pope Leo XIII, and Thérèse was determined to ask the Holy Father for permission to enter the convent. She would appeal to the highest authority on earth, the Vicar of Christ. Encouraged by her sister Céline, she asked Pope Leo to let her "enter Carmel," despite her young age. "You will enter if God wills," the wise pope responded. Returning home, Thérèse waited and waited until she finally entered Carmel on April 9, 1888.

† Thérèse's boldness is impressive! We should be bold like her. Yet sometimes, even when we have the courage to act with similar boldness, we get discouraged if we don't get immediate results. Be bold and be patient! Trust in the Lord to act.

DAY 7

As a nun, Thérèse prayed with fervor and served with fidelity. Whether she was assigned to sweep the floor, wash the dishes, or teach the young nuns, Thérèse did all for the love of God. When she had to deal with difficult sisters, she made a point of being even more kind and generous to them so that she could better love Jesus in her "enemies." On June 9, 1895, she offered herself as a sacrificial victim to the merciful Love of God. Two years later, she died of tuberculosis. Not long before she died, she wrote, "I am not dying; I am entering life." She passed away saying, "My God, I love you."

† Thérèse's lasting legacy is faithfulness in the little things— household chores, kindness to her sisters, daily prayer. This faithfulness allowed her to approach death—the biggest thing—with peace and calm. Recommit to the little things in your life.

St. Francis of Assisi

Deacon, religious brother, and founder of the Franciscan orders

Patron saint of Italy, stowaways, ecology, and animals

FEAST DAY: October 4

DAY 1

One of today's most popular saints is Francis of Assisi. Francis's original name was Giovanni, but people started calling him Francis when he was young, apparently for some reason related to his father's business dealings in France. While Francis was always generous with the poor, he wasn't interested in his schoolwork or his father's business as a cloth merchant. He seems to have been spoiled by his parents—not unlike some young men today who, disinterested in school and business, find themselves in the college party scene with their lives financed by their parents.

† Offer a fast this week for young people stuck in the college party scene, missing out on the fulfillment that comes from focus, direction, and relationship with Jesus. Take a day to eat only one meal and two snacks, or if you can't fast, give up something else you like for a day—soft drinks, social media, or the like. Make this a prayer for them.

DAY 2

Francis *was* interested in fighting, and he had a talent for leadership. He joined Assisi's armed men in a battle against a neighboring town, Perugia. They lost. After being taken prisoner and contracting a fever, Francis began to think about his death and whether the life he had been living would truly lead to his happiness.

† There is an ancient Christian practice of reminding ourselves, in Latin, *Memento mori* ("Remember that you are going to die"). Remembering that our lives on this earth will one day end puts everything in perspective. Take some time today to imagine yourself on your deathbed. What kind of life do you want to have lived? Start pursuing it now.

DAY 3

Back in Assisi, Francis gave up the idea of a military career and began to live differently. His friends were surprised when he started speaking less thoughtlessly, dressing more plainly, and taking more time in prayer and solitude. During this time, he passed a poor leper while riding his horse and, disgusted by the man's appearance, went the other way. But then Francis came to his senses. He remembered the dignity of this other human being, rode back, embraced the leper, and gave him all the money he had.

† Although his conversion was beginning, Francis (like all of us) still had a long way to go. At first, he couldn't see through the leper's external appearances to see Christ. Who do you struggle to truly see as Christ? Maybe it's people who do something you find objectionable, people of a certain political party, or people who have a different skin color than yours. Today, say something loving to a person you struggle to truly see.

DAY 4

After a pilgrimage to Rome, Francis returned to Assisi. He was praying before the crucifix in the dilapidated chapel of St. Damiano when he heard the voice of Jesus saying to him, "Go, Francis, and repair my house, which as you see is falling into ruin." Taking Him literally, Francis began to rebuild the small chapel using his father's money. This caused so much conflict with his family that he found himself disinherited and destitute. But Francis wasn't upset. He embraced the situation. He even stripped off his clothes and returned them to his father as he left to follow Christ with his whole heart, soul, mind, and strength.

† Open your Bible today and meditate on Luke 10:1–12.

DAY 5

Others began to gather around Francis, impressed by his way of life—living in total poverty, dependent on God alone. Faithful and devout Christians, Francis and his small group of disciples eventually set out for Rome to ask Pope Innocent III to approve them as a new religious order. At first, Pope Innocent rudely rejected them. But, like Francis with the leper, the pope started to reconsider. He talked to his advisers and prayed to God.

† Pope Innocent III was humble enough to change his mind. He was willing to listen to others and, most importantly, to Jesus. Are you willing to change your mind? Think of an issue that causes controversy in your life. Do a little more research. Talk to people who actually know about it. And pray with an open mind.

DAY 6

God gave Pope Innocent III a dream in which his church, St. John Lateran in Rome, was about to crumble to the ground but was being held up by a little man dressed in brown rags: Francis of Assisi. Pope Innocent called back Francis and his companions, approved their way of life, and gave them permission to preach anywhere. Francis's vision had come true. He *was* rebuilding Jesus's Church, not with mortar and stones as he'd first thought, but with poverty, repentance, and holiness.

† Francis was called upon to sustain and rebuild the Church by radically living the Christian life. How can you contribute to the building up of the Church? Maybe it's by fasting. Maybe it's by serving the poor. Maybe it's by teaching. Ask Jesus in prayer, then boldly follow where you perceive Him to be leading you.

DAY 7

Francis was totally focused on Jesus and wanted everyone to follow Him with his or her whole heart. In 1212, a young woman named Clare came to Francis asking to join in this way of radically living the gospel. Francis arranged for Clare and her sister, Agnes, to join in the way, and the Poor Clare Sisters were born. Francis also took it upon himself to preach Christ to the Muslims in the Holy Land, where he was received with courtesy and respect. To this day, because of his peaceful and clear preaching of the Gospels, the Franciscan Friars care for the holy sites in the Holy Land, where they strive for good relations among Christians, Jews, and Muslims. Although Francis is (along with Anthony of Padua) patron saint of animals because of the times he preached to flocks of birds and other creatures, his clear focus and deep passion was always the salvation of souls.

† Francis was able to cooperate with and preach to anyone to spread the love of Christ. Open your Bible today and pray with Galatians 3:25-29.

St. Teresa of Ávila

Virgin and Doctor of the Church

Patron saint of Spain, sick people, people ridiculed for their piety, lace makers, and religious brothers and sisters

FEAST DAY: October 15

DAY 1

Teresa of Ávila was born in Spain in 1515, and she was devout even as a child. Before she was nine years old, Teresa read about the lives of some heroic martyrs who had given their lives for Christ. Enthralled by their heroism, she longed to be a martyr herself and briefly ran away from home with the goal of dying a martyr's death and going to heaven. She told her parents, "I want to see God."

† Think back on all the saints you've met while reading this book. Whose example inspires you the most? Whose life is most like yours? Write some notes about those saints and put them in a place where you'll see them so that, like Teresa, you can be inspired by the holy men and women who have gone before us.

DAY 2

As a teenager, Teresa spent time living with her uncle, who introduced her to the Letters of St. Jerome, many of which were written to women striving to become saints. After reading these letters, Teresa knew she wanted to become a nun. Eventually, sneaking out of the house to avoid her father's disapproval, she entered the Carmelite Convent. When he learned what she had done, her father gave his permission, and Teresa became a nun at the age of 20.

† Books change our lives. Thoughts lead to feelings, feelings lead to actions, and actions lead to character. If we want to become saints, we must read good books and listen to good things. If you haven't already, ask people you admire what books they recommend. Make a list and get started.

DAY 3

In her life as a nun, Teresa received many graces from God in prayer. With her heart opened to grace by a severe sickness, she even received the deepest graces of mystical union with God. But for almost 20 years, she was more focused on the esteem of others than on Jesus. At times, she neglected mental prayer, also called contemplative prayer. What is mental prayer? As quoted in the *Catechism of the Catholic Church*, Teresa describes it as "nothing else than a close sharing between friends; it means taking time frequently to be alone with him who we know loves us."

† Take some time alone today. Set a timer for 5 or 10 minutes and, until that timer goes off, simply share with God what you're feeling or thinking. Then listen in silence. It's okay if you don't hear anything. Just be with Him.

DAY 4

Teresa gave the excuse that her sickness prevented her from engaging in mental prayer. But, as she would later write, "This reason of bodily weakness was not a sufficient cause to make me give over so good a thing, which requires not corporeal strength, but only love and custom. In the midst of sickness, the best of prayer may be made; and it is a mistake to think that it can only be made in solitude."

† Why are the saints often sick and suffering? For one thing, suffering is a gift of being with and like Jesus, who suffered for us. Another reason is that it teaches us the virtue of humility, realizing that, apart from Jesus, we can do nothing, which is the source of our true joy (see John 15:5, 11).

DAY 5

When she was 39 years old, things changed for Teresa. Often, she meditated at night on Jesus's agony in the Garden of Gethsemane. One night, she saw with new eyes a picture in the chapel that showed Jesus covered with the wounds and blood of His suffering. Falling to her knees, or maybe even prostrate on the floor, she begged Jesus to strengthen her so that she would never again offend Him. From then on, she lived a more devout life.

† Open your Bible to Luke 22:39-46. Ask Jesus to take you into His passion and, like He did for Teresa, give you the grace to never again offend Him. Then, when you fail, cast all your trust on God, who will send His angel to strengthen you.

DAY 6

Living a life of prayer and sacrifice, Teresa felt a great desire to be a saint herself and to help others become saints. She saw a need for reform in the convent. In prayer, Jesus affirmed this desire for reform, and she was given permission by His Church to found a convent that strictly observed the original Carmelite rule of life—the practices, daily schedule, and so on. But she'd barely started when she experienced persecution from both secular and religious authorities. Then, as the convent was being built, a wall fell, crushing the son of the donor who financed the project. But people brought the boy to Teresa, and as she prayed for him, he was miraculously healed.

† Teresa's bold obedience to the voice of Jesus required great trust. Turn to page 210 and pray the Litany of Trust today.

DAY 7

After various trials and successes, Teresa established this first convent under the patronage of St. Joseph. Later, she started other convents and, with the help of St. John of the Cross, whom she mentored, she founded monasteries of Carmelite brothers and fathers. All of this involved many sufferings for Teresa, John, and their friends. Yet others observed in amazement Teresa's constant joy, courage, humility, and gentleness even as she was slandered, reviled, and accused. She knew that it was God's work, not hers. She knew that she was in His will, so it did not matter what wicked men said (though perhaps it still hurt). She trusted in her Bridegroom, fulfilled her mission, and died a saint on October 4, 1582.

† Teresa's path to sainthood was a path of trust in the mercy of Jesus through many trials. Pray this prayer of hers, today and often: "Let nothing disturb you. Let nothing frighten you. All things are passing away: God never changes. Patience obtains all things. Whoever has God lacks nothing; God alone suffices."

St. Margaret Mary Alacoque

Virgin

Patron saint of those suffering with polio, those devoted to the Sacred Heart of Jesus, and those who have lost their parents

FEAST DAY: October 16

DAY 1

Born in 1647, Margaret is sometimes called the "Apostle of the Devotion to the Sacred Heart of Jesus." What exactly is devotion to the Sacred Heart of Jesus? The heart, the *Catechism* tells us, is "the depths of one's being, where the person decides for or against God." Jesus is God, so the depth of His being—His heart—is love (1 John 4:16).

† Open your Bible to 1 John 4:7-21. Think about how God loves you so much that He would take on a human body with a human heart. Ask Him for the strength to show that love to others.

DAY 2

In 1956, Pope Pius XII wrote an encyclical—a letter to the whole Church—about the Sacred Heart, which the *Catechism* uses to express the core of this devotion that Jesus revealed to Margaret Mary. "Jesus knew and loved us each and all during his life, his agony, and his Passion and gave himself up for each one of us: 'The Son of God . . . loved me and gave Himself for me' [Galatians 2:20]. He has loved us all with a human heart. For this reason, the Sacred Heart of Jesus, pierced by our sins and for our salvation [see John 19:34], 'is quite rightly considered the chief sign and symbol of that . . . love with which the divine Redeemer continually loves the eternal Father and all human beings' without exception."

✝ Our hearts should be like the heart of Jesus, filled with love for the Father and for our neighbors. Therefore, pray this prayer as many times as you can when you go about your day: "Jesus, meek and humble of heart, make my heart like unto Thine."

DAY 3

For many, the five wounds of Christ—from the spear that was thrust into His side and the nails that pierced His hands and His feet—are, as Pope Pius wrote, "the chief sign and symbol of that love." This was most certainly the case for Margaret. In her teen years, after she'd received her first Holy Communion, Jesus appeared to her to show her His presence and protection. He often appeared crucified on the cross.

✝ In every Catholic church, there should be a crucifix—a cross with the image of Christ crucified. Why do we continue to remember this horrible, bloody event in which we killed God? Because on the cross, God showed and continues to show us how much He loves us. Look at a crucifix today and think of the love it took for God to make that sacrifice. If you can, kiss each of the five wounds.

DAY 4

Even though Margaret was given mystical visions from God and had even, as a child, made a vow to become a nun when she was old enough, she chose instead to enter into the life of the world. One night, when she was coming home from a ball, Jesus appeared to her as He was during His scourging at the pillar, asking why, after He had given her the favor of visions and exceptional graces, she chose to put other things before a relationship with Him.

✝ Open your Bible to John 19:1–3. Meditate on Christ's great suffering in love for you and ask Him how you might, like Margaret, choose to be faithfully devoted to Him.

DAY 5

Margaret entered the Order of the Sisters of the Visitation of Holy Mary (founded not long before by St. Jane de Chantal and St. Francis de Sales, whom we met earlier) at 24 years old. Although she was living a very holy life, praying diligently and offering many sacrifices to Jesus (including choosing tasks and situations she didn't want), she wasn't seen as an exceptional nun. But she *was* an exceptional nun. She was good and simple or, in the words of one of her sisters, "humble, simple, and frank, but above all, kind and patient under sharp criticism and correction."

✝ The above virtues are great signs of true closeness to Jesus, whether or not others notice them. How can you practice these virtues in your life? Ask Jesus to help you.

DAY 6

When she'd been a nun for two or three years, Margaret began receiving the revelations of the Sacred Heart of Jesus. Jesus appeared to her from time to time over the course of 13 months, revealing the mystery of His Sacred Heart. She writes of one vision: "The Lord said to me, 'My Divine Heart is so passionately in love with humanity that it can no longer contain within itself the flames of its ardent love. It must pour them out through [you], and manifest itself to them with its precious treasures, which contain all the graces which they need to be saved.'"

✝ Gaze upon the image of the Sacred Heart of Jesus and think about His burning love for you. How does your love for your spouse or your children feel? Remember that burning in your heart and know that Jesus's love for you burns like that, but infinitely more.

DAY 7

Margaret faced plenty of persecution. Some thought her visions were delusions caused by a poor diet, and some of her sisters were openly against her. Some of her students' parents thought she was teaching against the Bible. Yet a Jesuit priest, now known as St. Claude de la Colombière, came into her life, recognized her visions, and supported her. Eventually, after many trials, Margaret's visions were proven legitimate, and she was even made assistant to the superior and placed in charge of the novice nuns in her convent. Margaret died at the age of 43. As she was receiving the last rites, she said, "I need nothing but God, and to lose myself in the heart of Jesus."

✝ Do you believe that Jesus is all you need? Open your Bible today and meditate on Psalm 63.

St. Martin of Tours

Bishop

Patron saint of France, soldiers (especially cavalry), conscientious objectors, winemakers, those who struggle with alcoholism, beggars, and tailors, among others

FEAST DAY: November 11

DAY 1

Martin was born into a Roman military family around AD 316, shortly after Constantine had come to power. As a child, Martin probably spent a lot of time in the military camps where, thanks to Constantine, Christianity was openly shared. Although his parents weren't Christian, Martin developed a deep love for God and, at 10 years old, asked to become a catechumen, preparing for baptism. At 12, still a catechumen, he desired to become a monk, but he was too young. Then, at 15, a new law required the sons of veterans to enroll in the army. Martin became a member of the cavalry and, although he could have had more, employed only one servant. He treated his servant as his equal, shunned the vices common to soldiers, lived a life of virtue, and cared for the poor.

† Sometimes we think our opportunities to become saints are limited by our circumstances. "If only I had more time to pray," we think. "If only I had better friends or a better community around me." Martin made no such excuses. He lived as close as he could to the life of a monk to which he felt called amid the duties of his life. May we follow his example!

DAY 2

In the northern parts of Europe, Roman soldiers wore heavy winter cloaks to shield them from the freezing temperatures. Once, when marching with fellow soldiers into the town of Amiens in Gaul (now France), Martin met a poor beggar, shivering and half-naked, at the city gates. Martin removed his cloak and cut it in half, giving one part to the beggar and keeping the other for himself. The next night, Jesus appeared to him in a dream wrapped in the very half-cloak Martin had given to the beggar. He said to a host of angels with Him, "Martin, yet a catechumen, has clothed me with this garment." Martin was baptized as soon as possible thereafter.

† Open your Bible to Matthew 25:31–46. If Jesus were to return today, how would you do in the Final Judgment? Ask Martin to pray for you and make a specific resolution about one way you will better love those in need. Don't forget all the times you do these works of mercy for your own children, spouse, and family members!

DAY 3

After his baptism, Martin wanted to leave the army immediately to pursue the life of a monk. But his friend and commanding officer convinced him to stay by committing to leave for the monastic life with him once their service ended. Soon, as a battle approached, the soldiers were given a financial bonus. Martin, thinking it would be wrong to take the money when he was planning on leaving so soon, asked if he could leave then and there, letting his money be given to someone else. He was accused of being a coward, but he responded by offering to be placed weaponless on the front line.

† Martin trusted in God. He didn't try to figure out a way to get what he wanted. He knew that God was calling him to leave the army, did everything in his power, and left the rest up to God. May we always be content doing everything reasonably in our power and leaving the rest up to Him. Turn to page 210 and pray the Litany of Trust today.

DAY 4

The night of Martin's offer, the enemies of the Romans sued for peace, the battle was avoided, and Martin was given permission to retire from the army. Freed from his military obligations, Martin set out to find himself a mentor in the Christian life. He went to learn from St. Hilary, bishop of Poitiers, who he'd heard was both holy and learned. But while Martin was visiting his family in Italy, Hilary was exiled from France, leaving Martin with no place to return. God provided for Martin with a holy priest in Italy who mentored him for a while. When Hilary was restored to his place in France, Martin went back and lived the life of a monk under Hilary's guidance.

† Martin knew he couldn't figure out how to be a disciple on his own. He needed someone to mentor him. Ask your mentor (if you have one), "Who's one person who mentored you? Tell me about that person."

DAY 5

Eventually, Martin became the bishop of Tours where, even as bishop, he continued to live as a monk, building a monastery two miles outside of the city. Although he lived at the monastery, he frequently visited all parts of his diocese to care for his people. On one occasion, Martin needed to speak with the emperor. He was denied entry two or three times, but after seven days of prayer and fasting, God inspired him to go boldly to the emperor, who this time received him and granted all of his needs for the church.

† Martin trusted in the power God grants when we fast and pray. How is your fasting? Commit to abstaining from meat or, at the very least, some other penance every Friday of the year to thank Jesus for His death on the cross and to pray for some grace from God, which you really need.

DAY 6

Martin's closeness to Jesus and knowledge of the Word of God made him very good at discerning spirits. Once, while he was praying, the devil appeared to him clothed in light, with royal robes, a golden crown, and many precious stones. This beautiful creature claimed he was Christ, but knowing that humility is the hallmark of the Lord, Martin paused to consider. Then he said, as Father Alban Butler recounts, "The Lord Jesus said not that he was to come clothed with purple, and crowned and adorned with a diadem. Nor will I ever believe him to be Christ who shall not come in the habit and figure in which Christ suffered, and who shall not bear the marks of the cross in his body." With that, the devil vanished, and Martin's cell was filled with a stench.

† Theologian and bishop Fulton Sheen once said that when the Antichrist comes, he and Christ will be almost identical; the only difference will be that the Antichrist has no wounds. Pray with a crucifix today. Meditate on the five wounds of Christ. Kiss the crucifix at each of the five wounds if you can.

DAY 7

Martin's last act as bishop of Tours, when he was about 80, was to travel to the outskirts of his diocese where there was a division among his clergy. After successfully bringing peace, he entered into his final sickness. His disciples asked, "Father, why do you forsake us? . . . The raving wolves will fall upon your flock." Moved with pity, he prayed, "Lord, if I am still necessary to thy people, I refuse no labor. Thy holy will be done." With this surrender to the will of God, Martin died on November 8, probably in the year 397.

† Turn to page 213 and pray the Surrender Novena all at once today, asking for surrender like Martin.

St. Frances Xavier Cabrini

Virgin and founder of the Missionary Sisters of the Sacred Heart of Jesus

Patron saint of immigrants, hospitals, and administrators

FEAST DAY: November 13

DAY 1

In March 2020, the state of Colorado established the first Monday of October as Cabrini Day in honor of this saint, whom Colorado Representative Adrienne Benavidez called "a great humanitarian" for her work in creating 67 schools, hospitals, and orphanages in North and South America. Cabrini Day is a paid state holiday, the first in the United States recognizing a woman.

† What an impact saintly women have had on the world! We have met so many of them so far—Catherine of Siena, Elizabeth Ann Seton, Mother Teresa, and more! Thank God today for the women in your life and the ways in which they exercise their spiritual motherhood in the footsteps of these great saints.

DAY 2

As a young child, Frances (then called Maria) was fascinated by the missions. Her father would read the family stories of missionaries that filled her imagination. She'd pretend her dolls were nuns, and when she visited her uncle, a priest who lived beside a canal, she'd send paper boats filled with violets off into the water, saying that the flowers were missionaries sailing off to proclaim Jesus Christ to the people of the world.

† Oftentimes, the first little saplings of our vocations can be seen when we're children. The playful imaginings of youth can easily mature into an adult's ardent zeal. Pay attention to the children in your life. Read them books and give them toys that foster the wholesome interests that are already there.

DAY 3

Frances accomplished great missionary work despite being plagued by ill health her entire life. Between the time when she was 13 and 18 years old, she spent five years at school with the Daughters of the Sacred Heart, earning a teaching certificate with honors. She applied to join the order, hoping to be sent to China as a missionary teacher, but she wasn't admitted because the sisters thought her health was too poor for missionary life.

† Perhaps her ill health wasn't an obstacle to her mission but rather a blessing. Perhaps it fostered in her the virtue of humility and dependence on God. Pray today all at once the Surrender Novena, found on page 213.

DAY 4

Frances's ill health and missionary zeal led her—at the suggestions of a Father Serrati and, later, the bishop of the city of Lodi—to reform an orphanage that wasn't serving the orphan girls as it should, and then to form a religious order of her own. She took the name Frances Xavier at the time of her vows, after St. Francis Xavier, the greatest missionary in the modern era.

† Frances was focused on the mission given to her by God. Open your Bible today and meditate on Luke 9:57–62. What moves you to look back? How can you be more focused on the field before you, entrusted to you by God Himself?

DAY 5

Italian immigrants (almost all Catholics) had found neither work nor welcome in the United States, and many were losing their faith, so Pope Leo XIII sent Mother Cabrini to care for them. On March 31, 1889, she arrived in New York from Italy with six members of the religious order she had founded, the Missionary Sisters of the Sacred Heart of Jesus. They began in the slums of New York, begging for money to open an orphanage, then a hospital.

† Although these immigrants were discriminated against by their new neighbors, Frances chose to be a neighbor to them. Open your Bible to Luke 10:25–37. Meditating on the story of the Good Samaritan, how can you better love your neighbor, especially those in your community who are immigrants?

DAY 6

Our Lord commands that we, His disciples, be "wise as serpents and innocent as doves" (Matthew 10:16). Frances surely fulfilled this command. She bought property, raised funds, and negotiated business deals, all for the sake of loving her neighbor. She built hospitals, schools, orphanages, and convents in Chicago, New Orleans, Philadelphia, Los Angeles, Seattle, Denver, and other US cities, as well as in Central America, South America, and Europe. Once, when the Missionary Sisters were remodeling a former hotel into a hospital in Chicago, contractors tried to cheat them. Mother Cabrini fired them, tucked up her habit, and spent a few weeks personally directing the workers.

† Frances lived with a holy boldness. She knew the mission God had given her—to serve the poor—and let nothing get in her way. May we live with this kind of holy boldness in obedience to God!

DAY 7

In 1909, Frances became a citizen of the United States. She was totally devoted to her mission. If her primary call, given by the pope, was to serve in America, then she would become an American. As Frederick Buechner wrote in *Wishful Thinking*, "The place where God calls you to is the place where your deep gladness and the world's deep hunger coincide." Frances's desire for her mission and her great administrative skills led her to the care of an innumerable number of girls and boys, immigrants and natives, Europeans and Americans. Thanks be to God that she was willing to respond to the world's hunger!

† Pray today—perhaps a decade of the rosary—for those who hold administrative positions in the Church: bishops, pastors, religious superiors, and the rest. Pray that they might be blessed with Frances's skill and courage to serve God's people well.

St. Catherine of Alexandria

Virgin and martyr

Patron saint of unmarried girls, lawyers, philosophers, apologists, librarians, archivists, and scholars, among others

FEAST DAY: November 25

DAY 1

Connected to the birthplace of Jesus in Bethlehem is the Roman Catholic Church of St. Catherine of Alexandria. Who is the saint asked to watch over such an important place? There's a lot of debate about which stories of her life are true, but Catherine is said to be the daughter of Constus, the governor of Alexandria in Egypt during the late third and early fourth centuries. Although its famous library had lost prestige by then, the wealth of books and scholars in the city trained Catherine's precocious mind.

† Today, the internet gives us access to great knowledge and some of the world's best teachers. How well are you using the internet? Resolve to use this gift to form your mind and become a saint.

DAY 2

A young woman of great knowledge, beauty, and holiness, Catherine attracted suitors from across the Roman Empire. She rejected all of them, however, telling her parents that she would only marry someone who surpassed her own nobility, wealth, intelligence, and good looks. Her mother, secretly a Christian, sent her to the local priest (living in secret), who told her of such a man: "His countenance is more radiant than the shining of the sun, and all of creation is governed by His wisdom. His riches are given to all the nations of the world, yet they never diminish. His compassion is unequaled." Instructing her to ask the Mother of God for prayers, he assured her that her desire would be granted.

† Catherine would not settle. She knew—or thought she knew—the kind of life she wanted. Then she worked and prayed that God might show her the way and grant her desires. May we do the same!

DAY 3

Praying one night, Catherine saw a vision of Mary holding Jesus, who said that He could not gaze upon her until she gave up her impiety. Distressed, Catherine returned to the priest to learn what she was supposed to do. The priest instructed her in the faith and encouraged her to continue to live a life of virtue and prayer. Then he baptized her. Cleansed of her sins and made a daughter of God, she received another vision. This time, Jesus looked upon her with great love and gave her a ring as a sign of her marriage—not to a man of earth, but to Himself.

† God answered Catherine's prayer, but not in the way she expected. Are we prepared to receive God's answers to our prayers, even when they're not what we're expecting? If we are, we will receive, like Catherine, even more joy than we imagined.

DAY 4

When Emperor Maxentius came to Alexandria for a pagan festival, he began to make human sacrifices of Christians in the arena. With prodigious intellect and fiery zeal, Catherine approached the emperor, declaring her faith in God and arguing for the truth of Christianity. Enthralled by her audacity, intelligence, and beauty, Maxentius summoned 50 learned men to debate with 18-year-old Catherine. Her arguments defeated them all. Some even converted to Christianity then and there, and were subsequently burned alive as martyrs on the spot. Catherine was thrown into prison.

† How many were converted by Catherine's boldness, holiness, and intelligence taken together! What do you do to train your mind? Open your Bible today to 1 Peter 3:13–17 and ask Jesus for the virtues of zeal, courage, and dedication to your Christian studies.

DAY 5

In prison, Catherine is said to have been cared for by angels and favored with a vision from Jesus encouraging her to be brave in her coming martyrdom. During her night in prison, Empress Valeria Maximilla, the wife of Maxentius, came to visit her, along with the military commander Porphyrius and a group of soldiers. They were impressed by a seemingly supernatural glow about her face and learned from her about Christianity.

† Notice that Jesus did not come to take Catherine's suffering away, but to assure her that He was with her in it—much like the angel had come to Him in His agony before His own passion. Read Luke 22:39–53 and remember that Jesus is with you, too, in your times of suffering.

DAY 6

Brought to trial and encouraged to renounce Christ, Catherine refused and was sentenced to death. But when the wagon wheel on which she was to be murdered shattered at her touch, the empress, the military commander, and many soldiers confessed their own faith in Jesus Christ. They were immediately beheaded. Trying again to lead her into sin, Maxentius proposed marriage to her, but Catherine refused, publicly declaring that Jesus was her Bridegroom. With a prayer, she was beheaded and left this earth to rejoice with her Bridegroom forever.

† The histories of the martyrs remind us that there is more to life than this world. They remind us that our souls are immortal and that eternity is worth much more than fleeting earthly pleasures. May we, like Catherine, be focused on intimacy with Jesus rather than on the things of this world!

DAY 7

Upon her death, Catherine's body is said to have been taken by monks or angels to Mount Sinai, where it was rediscovered 500 years later. It is said that her body was found incorrupt, laid on a slab of granite impressed with her form, her hair still growing. An oil that came forth from her body filled the air with a lovely fragrance and is said to have produced many miracles of healing. Even today, pilgrims can make the difficult journey to the top of Mount Sinai. Although they're not allowed to see her body, they can receive rings that have been placed upon her relics, reminding them of the mystical marriage to Jesus that Catherine experienced in a special way and to which we are all called as human beings made for intimate communion with God.

† Open your Bible to Luke 19:41–44 and meditate on how much Jesus longs to be in relationship with you.

St. Juan Diego Cuauhtlatoatzin

Layperson

Patron saint of Indigenous peoples

FEAST DAY: December 9

DAY 1

We began our walk through the lives of the saints with Mary, Queen of All Saints. Now, near the end of our journey this year, we meet her again through Juan Diego. Juan Diego was the first Indigenous American to be canonized as a saint. Surnamed Cuauhtlatoatzin ("the talking eagle"), our saint was born in Cuautitlán, today part of Mexico City. Born in 1474, he was baptized at 50 years old. He lived as a Christian, striving for virtue and even assisting at weekday Mass.

† It's never too late to begin walking more intentionally along the path of holiness. Have you tried going to weekday Mass? Make a point to go to Mass at least one day in addition to Sunday for a couple of weeks. See how it affects your life.

DAY 2

As Juan Diego was walking to Mass on the morning of Saturday, December 9, 1531, he was surprised to hear singing from the hill of Tepeyac. As he wondered whether this beautiful music was part of a dream, he heard a gentle voice from the top of the hill: "Juan, my little one, Juan Diego." Reaching the top of the hill, he found a young lady of supernatural beauty, clothed with the sun and standing upon what appeared to be precious stones. The landscape around her seemed to be filled with radiance.

✝   Mary, it seems, brought heaven with her to the hill of Tepeyac. Open your Bible to Revelation 21:9-27. Peer into St. John's vision of heaven and ask Jesus—through the intercession of His Mother and of Juan Diego—to inflame your soul with a desire to be there with Him for all eternity.

DAY 3

"Know and understand well, you my most humble son," Mary said to Juan Diego that day, "that I am the ever-virgin Holy Mary, Mother of the True God for whom we live, of the Creator of all things, Lord of heaven and earth." She told him she wanted a temple built quickly on the spot so that she could "give all my love, compassion, help, and protection, because I am your merciful mother, to you, and to all the inhabitants on this land and all the rest who love me, invoke and confide in me . . . and remedy all their miseries, afflictions and sorrows."

✝   Mary is our mother who wants to help us. We must be humble like Juan Diego, desiring and asking for her help. Pray a decade of the rosary today, asking Mary to help you in your greatest need.

DAY 4

To show her Son's mercy to the people of Mexico, Mary asked Juan Diego to go to the bishop of Mexico, telling him all he had seen and heard. The bishop listened intently but didn't believe Juan Diego. Disheartened, Juan returned to Tepeyac and implored Mary to send someone more important or respected to the bishop. "[M]y youngest and dearest son," she told him, "know for sure that I do not lack servants and messengers to whom I can give the task of carrying out my words . . . But it is very necessary that you plead my cause and, with your help and through your mediation, that my will be fulfilled."

† It was Juan Diego's humility that made him the perfect vessel for God's message in that time and place. He exemplified Mary's words to her cousin Elizabeth: "[God] has put down the mighty from their thrones, and exalted those of low degree" (Luke 1:52). It takes humility, not worldly power, to become a saint.

DAY 5

On his next visit, the bishop asked Juan Diego for a sign that the apparition was really the Blessed Virgin Mary. When Juan Diego told Mary this, she promised the sign if he'd return to Tepeyac the following day. That night, however, Juan Diego's uncle, with whom he lived, fell very ill. In the morning, he asked Juan Diego to travel to town to get the priest for the last rites. To avoid being delayed by Mary, Juan Diego took a path along the other side of the hill—but Mary walked down the hill to meet him. Hearing his worry for his uncle, Mary said to Juan Diego, "Let not your heart be disturbed. Do not fear that sickness, nor any other sickness or anguish. Am I not here, who is your Mother? Are you not under my protection? . . . Do not grieve nor be disturbed by anything. Do not be afflicted by the illness of your uncle, who will not die now of it. Be assured that he is now cured."

† Write down Mary's words and keep them with you. Use them as a prayer when you are worried or frightened.

DAY 6

At Mary's instruction, Juan Diego went to the top of a nearby hill, where he found flowers blooming, even though it was winter. He gathered them into his *tilma*, or cloak. She arranged them and commanded Juan Diego to show them only to the bishop. Arriving with some difficulty before the bishop, Juan Diego unfolded his cloak, revealing not only the flowers but also a miraculous image of Our Lady of Guadalupe. The bishop was convinced, and immediately a chapel was erected at Tepeyac and the miraculous image placed therein. Since then, Mexico has converted to Jesus Christ, and devotion to Him has spread by the powerful intercession of Our Lady of Guadalupe!

† Juan Diego was persistent in following the will of God as told to him by Mary. In a small way, he failed to trust that she would care for him, but when she told him she had healed his uncle, he immediately trusted her and followed her instructions. Persevere. Keep moving forward. Don't let little failures distract you from the goal.

DAY 7

Juan Diego received the bishop's permission to build a hut and live as a hermit near the first chapel where the *tilma* with Our Lady's miraculous image was kept. He devoted himself to prayer and to caring for the chapel, along with the pilgrims who came to pray before this miraculous work of God. When he died in 1548, he was buried in the same chapel. More than 400 years later, he was beatified and canonized in the Basilica of Our Lady of Guadalupe.

† The Guadalupe apparitions lasted for just four days out of Juan Diego's whole life. Most of his life was simple, humble, and, at least during his later years, prayerful. How can your life be more simple, humble, and prayerful?

St. Thomas Becket

Bishop and martyr

Patron saint of London; Exeter College at Oxford University; and diocesan bishops, priests, and deacons

FEAST DAY: December 29

DAY 1

Born in 1119 or 1120 and raised in a Christian home, Thomas was well educated in London, and then at Oxford and in Paris. At 21, having completed his studies (mostly in law and literature), he got a job as secretary to the city court in London, at which he was very successful. During this time, he got into hunting and hawking, which began to take up all of his free time and distract him from the service of God. One day, his hawk dove into a river in pursuit of a duck. Thomas, afraid of losing his hawk, dove in after it. He was swept down the river, saved only by the wheel of a water mill that seems to have stopped miraculously to save him. Grateful to God for saving his life, Thomas resolved to live with more devotion to God.

† In Thomas we see the virtue of gratitude. True gratitude actually changes our attitudes and our actions. For what are you grateful to God? Make a list today and think about how you can show that gratitude in your life.

DAY 2

Thomas was known to have great integrity, and he ended up working for Theobald, the archbishop of Canterbury, who had known his father. Theobald sent Thomas to Italy and France for further studies in canon law, then ordained him as a deacon, appointed him archdeacon of Canterbury (one of the most important positions in the church in England), and recommended him to the new king, Henry II, as lord chancellor of England, the second or third highest position in the government. At the time of his appointment, he was only around 36 years old.

† How are you with honesty and integrity? Do you always tell the truth? There's really no such thing as a "white lie." How about your business dealings? Are they honest? Evaluate the honesty of your life today.

DAY 3

Three years later, Theobald died while Henry and Thomas were away in Normandy. Henry wanted Thomas to become the next archbishop. Thomas responded, as Father Alban Butler recounted, "Should God permit me to be Archbishop of Canterbury, I should soon lose your majesty's favor, and the great affection with which you honor me would be changed into hatred. For . . . several things you do in prejudice of the inviolable rights of the church . . . make me fear you would require of me what I could not agree to." In other words, Thomas was warning the king that, if he were to become archbishop, he would stand up to the king's abuses of power. The king, however, paid no attention to these warnings. With the approval of church authorities, Thomas became archbishop of Canterbury on June 3, 1162.

† It is the duty of Christians to stand up against injustice. Ask for the intercession of Thomas Becket today as you pray for your bishop and your pastor, that they might courageously speak out and stand up against injustices wrought by the powerful.

DAY 4

As archbishop, Thomas lived much like a monk, exceptionally devoted to prayer and to the service of the poor. Not afraid of the powerful, he recovered some church property that had been stolen by wealthy Britons. Although he was rich, he ate simple food. He carried a copy of the Scriptures with him and took every break he could to read them.

† In every successful pastor, we see a primary focus on deep prayer and deep holiness. Read Mark 8:31–38 today and meditate on the overwhelming value of your soul.

DAY 5

There soon arose conflict, however, between the archbishop and the king. Henry, who had a role in appointing bishops, was intentionally delaying the process so he could collect those bishops' salaries for himself. On top of that, he wanted to require bishops to swear an oath to keep all the customs of his kingdom. Thomas wanted to add that they would do so "as far as was lawful, or consistent with duty." The king refused to consent, Thomas refused to swear, and the king condemned him, ordering all of his goods confiscated. Tempted by some to resign his office as archbishop, Thomas said that he would rather lay down his life than abandon the church.

† Obedience is the virtue by which we follow the legitimate directives of legitimate authority. But that doesn't mean we should follow immoral orders. How are you with obedience? Do you obey legitimate authority (like following the speed limit)? Do you disobey illegitimate directives (like dishonest business practices encouraged by a boss)? Ask Thomas to pray for you, that you might have courage to obey what's right and disobey what's wrong.

DAY 6

Although he wouldn't simply abandon his post, Thomas did humbly offer his resignation to the pope, who complimented his zeal and ordered him not to abandon his duties to God and His people. While Thomas spent some time at a monastery in France, the pope worked to restore the Church in England. Henry, however, was becoming more and more wicked. Eventually, Thomas was given a vision one night in prayer: He would be martyred by four agents of the king in his cathedral in Canterbury. In exile and seemingly abandoned by many, Thomas resolutely continued in his work for reform, righteousness, and religion in England, especially with the Christian's most powerful weapons: prayer and fasting.

† Thomas's humility is inspiring. Turn to page 217 and pray the Litany of Humility today.

DAY 7

After seven years away, Thomas resolved to return to England, closing his letter to King Henry with these words, as Butler recorded them: "With your majesty's leave I return to my church, perhaps to die there, and to hinder at least by my death its entire destruction. . . . But whether I live or die, I will always preserve inviolably that charity which I bear you in our Lord. And whatever may happen to me, I pray God to heap all his graces and good gifts on your majesty and on your children." On December 29, 1170, Thomas was confronted in the church by armed men accusing the archbishop of being a traitor. "Here I am, the archbishop," he replied, "but no traitor." Refusing to allow his church to become a fort or the scene of a battle, Thomas died praying for the men who brutally murdered him at the altar of St. Benedict. In response to Thomas's death, King Henry repented, and the Church was restored in England.

† Thomas died, as Jesus did, in peaceful defense of his people and their faith. Now he joins Jesus in the eternal joy of heaven. May we, too, follow in the footsteps of the saints and meet together in the eternal joy of heaven.

PRAYERS

LITANY OF TRUST

This prayer is written by Sister Faustina Maria Pia, SV, of the Sisters of Life.

From the belief that I have to earn Your love

Deliver me, Jesus.

From the fear that I am unlovable

Deliver me, Jesus.

From the false security that I have what it takes

Deliver me, Jesus.

From the fear that trusting You will leave me more destitute

Deliver me, Jesus.

From all suspicion of Your words and promises

Deliver me, Jesus.

From the rebellion against childlike dependency on You

Deliver me, Jesus.

From refusals and reluctances in accepting Your will

Deliver me, Jesus.

From anxiety about the future

Deliver me, Jesus.

From resentment or excessive preoccupation with the past

Deliver me, Jesus.

From restless self-seeking in the present moment

Deliver me, Jesus.

From disbelief in Your love and presence

Deliver me, Jesus.

From the fear of being asked to give more than I have

Deliver me, Jesus.

From the belief that my life has no meaning or worth

Deliver me, Jesus.

From the fear of what love demands

Deliver me, Jesus.

From discouragement

Deliver me, Jesus.

* * *

That You are continually holding me, sustaining me, loving me

Jesus, I trust in You.

That Your love goes deeper than my sins and failings and transforms me

Jesus, I trust in You.

That not knowing what tomorrow brings is an invitation to lean on You

Jesus, I trust in You.

That You are with me in my suffering

Jesus, I trust in You.

That my suffering, united to Your own, will bear fruit in this life and the next

Jesus, I trust in You.

That You will not leave me orphan, that You are present in Your Church

Jesus, I trust in You.

That Your plan is better than anything else

Jesus, I trust in You.

That You always hear me and in Your goodness always respond to me

Jesus, I trust in You.

That You give me the grace to accept forgiveness and to forgive others

Jesus, I trust in You.

That You give me all the strength I need for what is asked

Jesus, I trust in You.

That my life is a gift

Jesus, I trust in You.

That You will teach me to trust You

Jesus, I trust in You.

SURRENDER NOVENA

This novena was written by Father Dolindo Ruotolo as he perceived Jesus speaking to him in prayer.

Day 1

Why do you confuse yourselves by worrying? Leave the care of your affairs to Me and everything will be peaceful. I say to you in truth that every act of true, blind, complete surrender to Me produces the effect that you desire and resolves all difficult situations.

O Jesus, I surrender myself to You, take care of everything! (10 times)

Day 2

Surrender to Me does not mean to fret, to be upset, or to lose hope, nor does it mean offering to Me a worried prayer asking Me to follow you and change your worry into prayer. It is against this surrender, deeply against it, to worry, to be nervous and to desire to think about the consequences of anything. It is like the confusion that children feel when they ask their mother to see to their needs, and then try to take care of those needs for themselves so that their childlike efforts get in their mother's way.

Surrender means to placidly close the eyes of the soul, to turn away from thoughts of tribulation and to put yourself in My care, so that only I act, saying "You take care of it."

O Jesus, I surrender myself to You, take care of everything! (10 times)

Day 3

How many things I do when the soul, in so much spiritual and material need, turns to Me, looks at Me and says to Me, "You take care of it," then closes its eyes and rests. In pain you pray for Me to act, but that I act in the way you want. You do not turn to Me, instead, you want Me to adapt your ideas. You are not sick people who ask the doctor to cure you, but rather sick people who tell the doctor how to.

So do not act this way, but pray as I taught you in the Our Father: "Hallowed be thy Name," that is, be glorified in My need. "Thy kingdom come," that is, let all that is in us and in the world be in accord with Your kingdom. "Thy will be done on earth as it is in heaven," that is, in our need, decide as You see fit for our temporal and eternal life. If you say to Me truly: "Thy will be done," which is the same as saying: "You take care of it," I will intervene with all My omnipotence, and I will resolve the most difficult situations.

O Jesus, I surrender myself to You, take care of everything! (10 times)

Day 4

You see evil growing instead of weakening? Do not worry. Close your eyes and say to Me with faith: "Thy will be done. You take care of it." I say to you that I will take care of it, and that I will intervene as does a doctor and I will accomplish miracles when they are needed. Do you see that the sick person is getting worse? Do not be upset, but close your eyes and say, "You take care of it." I say to you that I will take care of it, and that there is no medicine more powerful than My loving intervention. By My love, I promise this to you.

O Jesus, I surrender myself to You, take care of everything! (10 times)

Day 5

And when I must lead you on a path different from the one you see, I will prepare you; I will carry you in My arms; I will let you find yourself, like children who have fallen asleep in their mother's arms, on the other bank of the river. What troubles you and hurts you immensely are your reason, your thoughts and worry, and your desire at all costs to deal with what afflicts you.

O Jesus, I surrender myself to You, take care of everything! (10 times)

Day 6

You are sleepless; you want to judge everything, direct everything, and see to everything; and you surrender to human strength, or worse—to men themselves, trusting in their intervention—this is what hinders My words and my views. Oh how much I wish from you this surrender, to help you; and how I suffer when I see you so agitated! Satan tries to do exactly this: to agitate you and to remove you from My protection and to throw you into the jaws of human initiative. So, trust only in Me, rest in Me, surrender to Me in everything.

O Jesus, I surrender myself to You, take care of everything! (10 times)

Day 7

I perform miracles in proportion to your full surrender to Me and to your not thinking of yourselves. I sow treasure troves of graces when you are in the deepest poverty. No person of reason, no thinker, has ever performed miracles, not even among the saints. He does divine works whosoever surrenders to God. So don't think about it any more, because your mind is acute and for you it is very hard to see evil and to trust in Me and to not think of yourself. Do this for all your needs, do this all of you and you will see great continual silent miracles. I will take care of things, I promise this to you.

O Jesus, I surrender myself to You, take care of everything! (10 times)

Day 8

Close your eyes and let yourself be carried away on the flowing current of My grace; close your eyes and do not think of the present, turning your thoughts away from the future just as you would from temptation. Repose in Me, believing in My goodness, and I promise you by My love that if you say "You take care of it" I will take care of it all; I will console you, liberate you and guide you.

O Jesus, I surrender myself to You, take care of everything! (10 times)

Day 9

Pray always in readiness to surrender, and you will receive from it great peace and great rewards, even when I confer on you the grace of immolation, of repentance, and of love. Then what does suffering matter? It seems impossible to you? Close your eyes and say with all your soul, "Jesus, you take care of it." Do not be afraid, I will take care of things and you will bless My name by humbling yourself. A thousand prayers cannot equal one single act of surrender, remember this well. There is no novena more effective than this.

O Jesus, I surrender myself to You, take care of everything! (10 times)

To be prayed as the last of each day's prayers:

Mother, I am yours now and forever.

Through you and with you

I always want to belong

completely to Jesus.

LITANY OF HUMILITY

This contemporary version of the prayer is by Servant of God Raphael Cardinal Merry del Val, secretary of state to Pope St. Pius X.

O Jesus! meek and humble of heart,

Hear me.

From the desire of being esteemed,

Deliver me, Jesus.

From the desire of being loved . . .

From the desire of being extolled . . .

From the desire of being honored . . .

From the desire of being praised . . .

From the desire of being preferred to others . . .

From the desire of being consulted . . .

From the desire of being approved . . .

From the fear of being humiliated . . .

Deliver me, Jesus

From the fear of being despised . . .

From the fear of suffering rebukes . . .

From the fear of being calumniated . . .

From the fear of being forgotten . . .

From the fear of being ridiculed . . .

From the fear of being wronged . . .

From the fear of being suspected . . .

That others may be loved more than I,

Jesus, grant me the grace to desire it.

That others may be esteemed more than I . . .

That, in the opinion of the world, others may increase and I may decrease . . .

That others may be chosen and I set aside . . .

That others may be praised and I unnoticed . . .

That others may be preferred to me in everything . . .

That others may become holier than I, provided that I may become as holy as I should . . .

PRAYER TO ST. MICHAEL

This prayer was written by Pope Leo XIII.

St. Michael the Archangel,

defend us in battle.

Be our protection against the wickedness and snares of
the Devil.

May God rebuke him, we humbly pray,

and do thou,

O Prince of the heavenly hosts,

by the power of God,

thrust into hell Satan,

and all the evil spirits,

who prowl about the world

seeking the ruin of souls.

Amen.

GUARDIAN ANGEL PRAYER

Angel of God, my guardian dear,

To whom God's love commits me here,

Ever this day be at my side,

To light and guard, to rule and guide.

Amen.

Resources

THE BIBLE

The Bible is an obvious resource for growing in relationship with Jesus. But how should you read the Bible? Where do you begin? I recommend starting with the Gospels in the Word on Fire Bible (WordOnFire.org/bible), which is made for people approaching the Bible for the first time.

YouVersion is, at the time of this publication, an excellent app which has both the text and audio of most of the Bible available for free.

MOVIES AND TELEVISION

The Passion of the Christ (2004) is an excellent depiction of the suffering and death of Jesus.

The Chosen is an excellent streaming series that focuses on the life of biblical saints who knew Jesus as He walked in the flesh. While the genre is historical fiction, the dynamics of the saints' encounters with Jesus are incredibly true to life.

ONLINE RESOURCES

Each saint's page on Wikipedia, while it cannot always be taken to be completely accurate, offers basic facts, a workable bibliography, and a good starting point for learning about a particular saint.

Good and detailed information on many saints can be found in the *Catholic Encyclopedia*, available at NewAdvent.org/cathen.

Strive (Strive21.com) is a free, anonymous 21-day challenge for those who struggle with pornography, one of the greatest obstacles to being a saint today.

BOOKS

Nonfiction

The Roman Catholic *Liturgy of the Hours* provides a very good and very short reading for each saint's feast day in its *Office of Readings*.

Pope St. John Paul II gives papal advice for each of us on living a saintly life today in *Christifideles Laici*, which can also be found on the Vatican website.

Many of our saintly stories speak of their discerning a vocation. Two books that are great aids in listening to God's voice when making significant life choices are *Pray, Decide, and Don't Worry: Five Steps to Discerning God's Will* by Bobby and Jackie Angel and *God's Voice Within: The Ignatian Way to Discover God's Will* by Father Mark E. Thibodeaux, SJ.

Fiction

The *Sword and Serpent* trilogy by Taylor Marshall is an excellent work of historical fiction, featuring saints such as St. George, St. Catherine of Alexandria, St. Christopher, and St. Nicholas.

The Lord of the Rings by J. R. R. Tolkien displays saintly virtues that can help us live like the saints.

The Chronicles of Narnia by C. S. Lewis also displays saintly virtues.

References

Aristotle. *Nicomachean Ethics*. Edited by Hugh Tredennick. Translated by J. A. K. Thomson. New York: Penguin Classics, 2004.

Arnald of Sarrant. *Chronicle of the Twenty-Four Generals of the Order of Friars Minor*. Translated by Noel Muscat, OFM. Malta: TAU Franciscan Communications, 2010.

Basil the Great. *On the Human Condition*. Popular Patristics Series, Number 30. Translated by Nonna Verna Harrison. Crestwood, NY: St. Vladimir's Seminary Press, 2005.

Benedict XVI. "Apostolic Letter Proclaiming Saint Hildegard of Bingen, Professed Nun of the Order of Saint Benedict, a Doctor of the Universal Church." *The Holy See*. October 7, 2012. Accessed July 16, 2020. Vatican.va/content/benedict-xvi/en /apost_letters/documents/hf_ben-xvi_apl_20121007_ildegarda -bingen.html.

———. "Saint Teresa of Avila." *The Holy See*. February 2, 2011. w2.Vatican.va/content/benedict-xvi/en/audiences/2011 /documents/hf_ben-xvi_aud_20110202.html.

Benedictine Monks of St. Augustine's Abby, Ramsgate, eds. *The Book of Saints: A Dictionary of Servants of God Canonised by the Catholic Church: Extracted from the Roman & Other Martyrologies*. London: A. & C. Black, 1921.

Bojaxhiu, Mary Teresa. *A Life for God: Mother Teresa Treasury*. Edited by Lavonne Neff. New York: HarperCollins, 1996.

Buechner, Frederick. *Wishful Thinking: A Seeker's ABC*. New York: HarperOne, 1993.

Butler, Rev. Alban. *The Lives of the Fathers, Martyrs, and other Principal Saints*. New York: P. J. Kenedy, 1903.

Cannon, Mae Elise. *Just Spirituality: How Faith Practices Fuel Social Action*. Downers Grove, IL: IVP Books, 2013.

Catechism of the Catholic Church. Washington, DC: United States Catholic Conference, 2000.

Catherine of Siena. *Catherine of Siena: The Dialogue*. Translated by Suzanne Noffke, OP. New York: Paulist Press, 1980.

Center for the Study of Global Christianity at Gordon-Conwell
Theological Seminary. "Status of Global Christianity, 2020,
in the Context of 1900–2050." 2020. GordonConwell.edu
/center-for-global-christianity/wp-content/uploads/sites/13
/2020/02/Status-of-Global-Christianity-2020.pdf.

Chrysostom, John. "Homily II on 1 Thessalonians." *Nicene
and Post-Nicene Fathers: First Series* 13, edited by Philip Schaff, 331.
New York: Cosimo Classics, 2007.

Cihak, Fr. John. "St. John Vianney's Pastoral Plan." *Ignatius Insight.*
Accessed July 3, 2020. IgnatiusInsight.com
/features2009/jcihak_cureofarshpr_june09.asp.

Clucas, Joan Graff. *Mother Teresa.* New York: Chelsea House
Publications, 1988.

Commission for the Franciscan Intellectual Tradition. "A Letter
to Brother Anthony of Padua." Accessed July 3, 2020.
FranciscanTradition.org/francis-of-assisi-early-documents
/writings-of-francis/a-letter-to-brother-anthony-of-padua
/123-fa-ed-1-page-107.

Crossroads Initiative. "Mary Magdalene—Gregory the Great."
July 21, 2019. CrossroadsInitiative.com/media/articles
/mary-magdalene.

Dominican Sisters of Saint Cecilia. "St. Rose of Lima." Accessed July 3,
2020. NashvilleDominican.org/community/our
-dominican-heritage/our-saints-and-blesseds/st-rose-lima.

Doyle-Nelson, Theresa. "Get to Know the Little-Known Anna the Proph-
etess." *National Catholic Register.* Feb. 3, 2018.
NCRegister.com/blog/tdoylenelson/get-to-know-the-little
-known-st.-anna-the-prophetess.

Ebrahimji, Alisha. "Colorado Will Replace Columbus Day with Cabrini
Day, the First Paid State Holiday Recognizing a Woman in the US."
CNN. March 11, 2020. CNN.com/2020/03/11/us
/colorado-columbus-day-cabrini-day-trnd/?hpt=ob
_blogfooterold.

Eusebius. *An Ecclesiastical History to the Twentieth Year of the Reign of
Constantine: Being the 324th of the Christian Era.* Translated by C. F.
Crusè. London: Samuel Bagster & Sons, 1847.

Fenner, F., D. A. Henderson, I. Arita, Z. Jezek, and I. D. Ladnyl. *Small-pox and Its Eradication*. WHO. 1998. Biotech.law.lsu.edu/blaw/bt/smallpox/who/red-book/index.htm.

Francis I. "Holy Mass and Canonization of Blessed Mother Teresa of Calcutta." *The Holy See*. September 4, 2016. w2.Vatican.va/content/francesco/en/homilies/2016/documents/papa-francesco_20160904_omelia-canonizzazione-madre-teresa.html.

———. "Pope at Urbi et Orbi: Full Text of His Meditation." *Vatican News*. March 27, 2020. VaticanNews.va/en/pope/news/2020-03/urbi-et-orbi-pope-coronavirus-prayer-blessing.html.

Franciscan Friars of the Immaculate. *A Handbook on Guadalupe*. Austin: University of Texas Press, 2001.

Franciscan Media. "Saint Margaret Mary Alacoque." Accessed July 3, 2020. FranciscanMedia.org/saint-margaret-mary-alacoque.

Gaitley, Michael E. *33 Days to Morning Glory: A Do-It-Yourself Retreat in Preparation for Marian Consecration*. Stockbridge, MA: Marian Press, 2011.

Gregory I. *The Book of Pastoral Rule*. Translated by George E. Demacopoulos. Yonkers, New York: St. Vladimir's Seminary Press, 2007.

———. "Homily 26 on the Gospels." Patristic Bible Commentary. Accessed July 3, 2020. sites.Google.com/site/aquinasstudybible/home/gospel-of-john-commentary/gregory-the-great-homily-26-on-the-gospels.

———. "Homily 33 on the Gospels." Patristic Bible Commentary. Accessed July 3, 2020. sites.Google.com/site/aquinasstudybible/home/luke-commentary/gregory-the-great-homily-33-on-the-gospels.

Henderson, Br. Silas, SDS. "These Are the Words Jesus Said to Renew Devotion to His Sacred Heart." *Aleteia*. October 16, 2018. Aleteia.org/2018/10/16/these-are-the-words-jesus-said-to-renew-devotion-to-his-sacred-heart.

Hindi, Saja. "Columbus Day No Longer a State Holiday in Colorado: Governor Signs Bill Replacing Holiday with Cabrini Day." *Denver Post*. March 20, 2020. DenverPost.com/2020/03/20/colorado-columbus-day-cabrini.

International Commission on English in the Liturgy. *Liturgy of the Hours*. New Jersey: Catholic Book Publishing, 1990.

John Paul II. "Apostolic Letter Proclaiming St. Therese a Doctor of the Church." Society of the Little Flower. Accessed July 3, 2020. Little-Flower.org/therese/doctor-of-the-church/apostolic -letter-full-text.

———. "Sollicitudo Rei Socialis." *The Holy See*. December 30, 1987. Vatican.va/content/john-paul-ii/en/encyclicals/documents /hf_jp-ii_enc_30121987_sollicitudo-rei-socialis.html.

Koppedrayer, K. I. "The Making of the First Iroquois Virgin: Early Jesuit Biographies of the Blessed Kateri Tekakwitha." *Ethnohistory* 40, no. 2 (Spring 1993): 277–306. doi:10.2307 /482204.

Landy, Thomas M. "Ugandan Martyrs' Feast." *Catholics & Cultures*. Accessed July 3, 2020. CatholicsAndCultures.org/uganda /shrines-pilgrimage/martyrs-shrine-feast-namugongo.

Langr, Chloe. "Could Alessandro Serenelli Be the Future Patron of Porn Addicts?" *Epic Pew*. July 6, 2017. EpicPew.com /alessandroserenellimariagoretti.

Leo XIII. "Prayer to Saint Michael." Loyola Press. Accessed July 6, 2020. LoyolaPress.com/catholic-resources/prayer /traditional-catholic-prayers/saints-prayers/prayer-to-st -michael.

Mark, Joshua J. "Hildegard of Bingen." *Ancient History Encyclopedia*. May 30, 2019. Ancient.eu/Hildegard_of_Bingen.

Merlo, Francesca. "The story of Our Lady of Guadalupe." *Vatican News*. December 11, 2018. VaticanNews.va/en/church/news /2018-12/our-lady-of-guadaloupe-feast-day-mexico-americas .html.

Merry del Val, Rafael. "Litany of Humility." In *A Prayerbook of Favorite Litanies*, compiled by Albert J. Hebert. Gastonia, NC: St. Benedict Press, 2011.

Mitch, Curtis and Edward Sri. *The Gospel of Matthew: Catholic Commentary on Sacred Scripture*. Ada, MI: Baker Academic, 2010.

National Kateri Tekakwitha Shrine. "Kateri's Pathway to Sainthood." Accessed July 3, 2020. web.Archive.org/web /20170310061442/http://katerishrine.com/kateri.html.

Newman, Barbara. "Hildegard of Bingen: Visions and Validation." *Church History: Studies in Christianity and Culture* 54, no. 2 (1985). doi:10.2307/3167233.

Orthodox Church in America. "Great Martyr Catherine of Alexandria." Accessed July 3, 2020. OCA.org/saints/lives /2015/11/24/103382-great-martyr-catherine-of-alexandria.

Paul VI. "Dogmatic Constitution on the Church, Lumen Gentium, Solemnly Promulgated by His Holiness Pope Paul VI on November 21, 1964." *The Holy See*. November 21, 1964. Vatican.va/archive/hist_councils/ii_vatican_council/documents /vat-ii_const_19641121_lumen-gentium_en.html.

———. "Homily for the Canonization of Elizabeth Ann Seton." *The Holy See*. September 14, 1975. Vatican.va/content/paul-vi/en /homilies/1975/documents/hf_p-vi_hom_19750914.html.

Perry, Norman, OFM. "Devotion to St. Anthony of Padua." American Catholic. Accessed July 3, 2020. web.Archive .org/web/20001208090300/http://www.americancatholic .org/Features/Anthony/0-86716-202-3_np.asp.

Pia, Sr. Faustina Maria, SV. "The Litany of Trust." Sisters of Life. Accessed July 6, 2020. SistersOfLife.org/wp-content /uploads/2019/07/Mobile-Litany-of-Trust.pdf.

Pius XII. "Haurietis Aquas: On Devotion to the Sacred Heart." *The Holy See*. May 15, 1956. Vatican.va/content/pius-xii/en /encyclicals/documents/hf_p-xii_enc_15051956_haurietis -aquas.html.

Regnum Christi. "St. José Sánchez del Río: A Soldier for Jesus." November 11, 2019. RegnumChristi.org/en/st-jose-sanchez -del-rio-a-soldier-for-jesus.

Rothman, Lily. "How Mother Cabrini Became the First American Saint." *TIME*. July 6, 2016. TIME.com/4380994/frances -cabrini-first-american-saint.

Ruotolo, Fr. Dolindo. "Surrender Novena." Divine Will. Accessed July 6, 2020. DivineWillUK.com/surrender-novena.

"Saint Frances Xavier Cabrini: Virgin, Foundress—1850-1917." Eternal Word Television Network. Excerpt from *Lives of Saints with Excerpts from Their Writings*. New York: John J. Crawley, 1954. Accessed July 3, 2020. web.Archive.org/web

/20190530180427/http://www.ewtn.com/library/MARY
/CABRINI.HTM.

Sanctuary of Corinaldo. "Maria's Life." Accessed July 3, 2020.
SantaMariaGoretti.it/wp/marias-life/#famiglia.

Schaff, Philip and Henry Wace, eds. *Nicene and Post-Nicene Fathers:
Second Series*, vols. 1–7. New York: The Christian
Literature Company, 1898.

Society of Saint Pius X. "'I Am Your Mother': Our Lady of
Guadalupe." December 11, 2014. SSPX.org/en/i-am-your
-mother-lady-of-guadalupe.

Synodus Episcoporum. "St. Charles Lwanga and Companions."
Accessed July 3, 2020. Synod.va/content/synod2018/en
/youth-testimonies/st—charles-lwanga-and-companions
—martyrs-of-uganda.html.

Tertullian. "Apologeticum." Tertullian.org. Accessed July 8, 2020.
Tertullian.org/works/apologeticum.htm.

Thérèse of Lisieux. *The Autobiography of Saint Thérèse of Lisieux.*
Translated by John Beevers. New York: Random House, 2011.

"The Trial of Joan of Arc." Translated by Régine Pernoud. Accessed July
8, 2020. college.Cengage.com/history
/primary_sources/west/the_trial_joan_of_arc.htm.

University of Dayton. "All About Mary: Nican Mopohua."
Accessed July 3, 2020. UDayton.edu/imri/mary/n/nican
-mopohua.php.

Vatican, The. "Josephine Bakhita (1869–1947)." *The Holy See.* Accessed
July 3, 2020. Vatican.va/news_services/liturgy
/saints/ns_lit_doc_20001001_giuseppina-bakhita_en.html.

———. "Juan Diego Cuauhtlatoatzin (1474–1548)." Accessed
July 3, 2020. Vatican.va/news_services/liturgy/saints
/ns_lit_doc_20020731_juan-diego_en.html.

———. "Teresa Benedict of the Cross Edith Stein (1891–1942)."
The Holy See. Accessed July 16, 2020. Vatican.va/news_services
/liturgy/saints/ns_lit_doc_19981011_edith_stein_en.html.

Vatican News. "Mother Theresa of Calcutta." Accessed July 3, 2020.
VaticanNews.va/en/saints/09/05/s--mother-theresa-of
-calcutta.html.

Zanini, Roberto Italo. *Bakhita: From Slave to Saint.* San Francisco: Ignatius Press, 2013.

Index

F

L

Last Supper, 38
Lawrence, St., 137–140
Lazarus, 105, 122–124
Leander (bishop), 58
Legnani, Callisto, 26
Leo XIII (Pope), 35, 85, 176, 195, 219
Lily of the Mohawks, 115
The Lion King (film), 53
Litany of Humility (prayer), 217–218
Litany of Trust (prayer), 210–212
Liturgy of the Hours, 75
Lives of the Saints (Butler), 87, 138
Louis, St., 173
Lucifer, 170
Luke, St., 118, 165, 167
Luke 1:28, 3
Luke 1:42, 3
Luke 1:46–55, 171
Luke 1:52, 203
Luke 2:22–24, 21
Luke 2:25, 21, 22
Luke 2:30, 23
Luke 2:32, 23
Luke 2:36, 24
Luke 2:37, 24
Luke 5:16, 131
Luke 5:29, 165
Luke 7:36–50, 119
Luke 7:38, 118
Luke 7:47, 119
Luke 7:50, 119
Luke 8:1–3, 119
Luke 9:23, 79
Luke 9:59–62, 154, 195
Luke 10, 120
Luke 10:1, 5
Luke 10:1–12, 79, 107, 179
Luke 10:1–17, 65
Luke 10:25–37, 195
Luke 10:38–42, 59, 72
Luke 10:40, 121
Luke 10:41–42, 96

Luke 10:42, 104
Luke 12:22, 122
Luke 12:48, 50
Luke 16:9–13, 140
Luke 19:41–44, 200
Luke 22:29–46, 68
Luke 22:39–46, 183
Luke 22:39–53, 199
Luke 22:54–62, 102

M

Macarius, St., 159
March 3, Katharine Drexel
(feast day), 33
March 7, Perpetua and Felicity
(feast day), 37
March 9, Frances of Rome
(feast day), 41
March 17, Patrick (feast day), 45
March 18, Cyril of Jerusalem
(feast day), 49
March 19, Joseph (feast day), 53
Margaret Mary Alacoque, St., 185–188
Maria Goretti, St., 109–112
Mark, St., 65–68, 118, 167, 168
Mark 3:13–19, 167
Mark 6:7, 5
Mark 8:31–38, 207
Martha, St., 121–124
Martin, Marie Françoise-Thérèse, 173
Martin of Tours, St., 189–192
Martins de Bulhões, Fernando, 93
Martyrdom, *ix*, 32, 40, 61, 63, 92, 95,
112, 138, 140, 199
Mary, Joseph as spouse of Virgin
Mary, 53–56
Mary, Queen of All Saints, 1–4, 201
Mary Magdalene, St., 82, 117–120, 121
Matthew, St., 165–168
Matthew 1:16, 53
Matthew 1:18–2:23, 2
Matthew 1:19, 55
Matthew 1:20–21, 55
Matthew 1:24, 56

Acknowledgments

A great publisher is a gift to a novice author—and also to an experienced one, I'm sure! From my first interactions with Matt Buonaguro to my extensive contact with Lauren O'Neal, I am very grateful to Rockridge Press for giving me a shot at my first book.

I am most grateful to Lauren for her precise editing, keen insights, and constant encouragement. Your patience with me as the 2020 COVID-19 pandemic wreaked havoc upon our initial schedule was a gift.

Over the past three years, I have preached many a homily on the life of this or that saint, during which I was unknowingly being prepared for this writing. Thank you to the people of St. Francis in Houma, Christ the Redeemer in Thibodaux, and Holy Cross in Morgan City for praying with me and praying for me over these past three years when I have been privileged to serve as a priest of Jesus Christ.

Finally, to my parents and my friends, who loved me through times of frustration as I stressed over this or that deadline, I could not be more grateful! I am a better man for being surrounded by such patient kindness.

O give thanks to the Lord, for he is good;

for his mercy endures for ever!

—Psalm 107:1

ABOUT THE AUTHOR

Father Brice Higginbotham is a Catholic priest for the Diocese of Houma-Thibodaux, in Louisana, where he currently serves as pastor of Holy Cross Parish and as chaplain for Central Catholic School. He also serves as a *censor librorum*, frequent consultant to the Office of Parish Support, media evangelist, and master of ceremonies. In the past, he has served as a parochial vicar, assistant vocations director, state police chaplain, and member of the Diocesan Presbyteral Council. Father Brice received his master's degree in theological studies from Notre Dame Seminary in New Orleans, Louisiana. He has published two articles in *Homiletic & Pastoral Review* and more than 60 catechetical videos in cooperation with the Diocese of Houma-Thibodaux's Offices of Parish Support and Communications, all of which are available on YouTube and Facebook.

Printed in the USA
CPSIA information can be obtained
at www.ICGtesting.com
LVHW051726241223
767315LV00002B/2